A guide to

LOUGH CORRIB'S

EARLY MONASTIC SITES

ANTHONY PREVITÉ

Published by Oldchapel Press

First published in 2010 by

Oldchapel Press
Oldchapel, Oughterard
Co. Galway, Republic of Ireland

www.oldchapelpress.net

© Text by Anthony Previté 2010

Anthony Previté has asserted his rights to be identified
as the author of this book.

© Maps courtesy of Connemara Publications 2010
Hand drawings and photography by the author unless otherwise stated.

The material in this book is protected by copyright law. Except as may be permitted by law, no part of the material may be reproduced (including by storage in a retrieval system) or transmitted in any form or by any means, adapted, rented or lent without the written permission of the copyright owners. Applications for permissions should be addressed to the publisher.

Cover Photo: Lough Corrib - photo courtesy of Jess Walsh

ISBN: 978-0-9560062-1-9

Layout and design by Connemara Publications, Clifden, Co. Galway
Printed in Ireland by Castle Print, Galway City

CONTENTS

“Ruins are not empty.
They are sacred places full of presence.”

John O’Donohue

Acknowledgements

Michael Curran, Killagoola, Moycullen, Brian Mulkerrins, Clydagh, Moycullen, and Paddy Healy, Portacarron, Oughterard, with gratitude for their valuable help with local knowledge and introduction to some of the sites.

My sincere thanks to Dave Hogan, Letterfrack, a cheerful and gifted historian, ecologist, musician, guide and language expert who generously led the way in editing the script and assisted me with the standardisation and interpretation of the Irish saints' and place names.

Michael Gibbons, archaeologist, Clifden, who has an endless ability to be constantly discovering new archaeological remains. With his abounding knowledge and infectious enthusiasm for his subject, I am grateful for his constant encouragement and for his professional scanning of the archaeological aspects of this book.

To my son Oliver, Moycullen, for his energetic ability in assisting to access the most impenetrable archaeological remains. Also for his photograph of the Cross of Cong taken at National Museum, Turlough.

Catherine Jennings, historian, Carna, for generously opening up to me some of her fascinating researches into the life of St Foillan and his foundation at Fosses-la-Ville.

Kathleen Villiers-Tuthill, historian, Clifden, has been described as a gem of Connemara and I am always grateful for her encouragement and for a specific honour she has done me in this work.

I am very grateful to my direct neighbour and photographer, Jess Walsh, Oughterard, for one of her pictures which now graces the front cover of this book. Lough Corrib is not an easy area to encapsulate in only one photograph but this one generates that sense of mystery and timelessness that belongs to all of it.

Much photography from others, to supplement my own efforts, has been very gratefully included and individually acknowledged, from Liam Donoghue, Headford, Fr John Musther, Northumbria, John Smyth, Galway (www.johnsmyth.ie), David P. Powell, Philadelphia, USA, and Dr. Andreas F. Borchert, Germany.

Many of these are aerial photos as many sites can only be appreciated from an altitude. In this regard I am particularly grateful to my friend Seamus Coughlan, Athenry, who so kindly flew me over some of these sites in his Piper Super Cub, whilst I leaned out of an open hatch nervously clutching my neighbour's high spec camera!

My thanks to Lol Hardiman, Clifden, for his hand drawn depiction of what the ancient and early oratory at Portacarron, Oughterard, might possibly have looked like.

To my wife Christina I am ever grateful for her keen eye in assisting with proof reading, her companionship on some of my excursions and her generous patience with me.

Noel Mannion and Catherine Lavoie, Connemara Publications, Clifden, are without doubt the most excellent of graphic designers and I am ever grateful for their true commitment to the work, their professionalism, skill, good humour, encouragement, attention to the smallest detail and for their plain, honest kindness and help. Without them this publication might never have come to fruition.

INTRODUCTION

Lough Corrib is that beautiful 45km stretch of inland waterway that reaches from the coastal city of Galway right into Connemara. At its widest point of 21km, this vast and ever-changing sheet of water, punctuated with 145 interesting islands (some say 365 for each day of the year!), is bordered by a wide variety of coastline and which country is home to the 31 early monastic sites referred to in this book. This watery highway would have been the main thoroughfare in those ancient times and with an area of 180 square kilometers is the second largest lake in Ireland. In the 4th century Brian Orbsen was King of Connacht and is the same that gave his name to the present day Lough Corrib, i.e., Lough Orbsen or Lough Orbs.

The saints of Ireland derive from the various *Tuatha*, tribes or peoples, who lived in Ireland. The vast majority of these saints lived during the 4th-10th centuries, a period in which Ireland was known as the "land of saints and scholars", and it produced many missionaries from that time. The introduction of Christianity into Ireland was during the end of the 4th century, and although its exact introduction is obscure, the strict ascetic nature of this early monasticism suggests strong connections to the Coptic monks from Egypt.

These origins and influences for the Early Monastic settlements to be found throughout our western shores, islands and inland waterways have been explored and described in my earlier book, *A Guide to Connemara's Early Christian Sites* published in 2008. That these origins came by the sea routes from the North African ascetic hermits (The Desert Fathers of the 3rd century AD) underlines the very skilled maritime life that was so well established across the oceans in those times. This Early Monastic life grew in Ireland from the 3rd-4th century until the 9th century when it was largely destroyed by the coming of the Vikings who laid waste to so much of the artwork, treasures and buildings that had begun to flourish. The maritime and hardy traditions of these early monks, together with their obviously strong religious fervour, then led them to migrate by various routes back to mainland Europe. There they established many religious houses and settlements which still exist today and in many cases the early saints connected with them are venerated and celebrated to a far higher extent than here in Ireland.

St Anthony the Great (251–285 AD) and his followers moved out from the Holy Lands across into North Africa where they practised this life of self-denial, and along with such as Clement of Alexandria, the Stylites and the Stoics, collectively became generally known as 'The Desert Fathers'. That many of the physical remains of these early Irish monastic settlements so often lie as abandoned or vandalised piles of stones or overgrown with ivy and thorn bushes, is a tragic reflection of the present day values we place on this important and significant era of our cultural, religious and architectural heritage. It is hoped that these little publications will help to raise an awareness and appreciation of this valuable inheritance with a view to it being preserved and perhaps further researched. Sir William Wilde commented strongly on this aspect in his work on Lough Corrib (1867):

'During past times here and elsewhere, religious fanaticism, and the ignorance and want of taste in the gentry and farming classes, or the mischievousness of peasant boys, injured many of our most beautiful sacred edifices; and now, when improved education among the former, and depopulation among the latter, have arrested these desecrations, weeds, brambles, and wild shrubs hold undisputed rule among the historic

landmarks of the past. Visiting the cultivated demesnes often located in the immediate vicinity of these Irish ruins, and admiring the carefully-shaven grass-plots and highly cultivated gardens and parterres, the antiquary cannot help wondering why a few pounds have not been expended upon the preservation of edifices once devoted to the service of religion, illustrative of the greatest architectural period of the country, and frequently containing the mausolea of the ancestors of their proprietors. And when, again, we see large sums of money expended on ugly unarchitectural structures for religious worship, we cannot help asking ourselves why the clergy of Ireland, no matter what their special persuasion may be, have done nothing to re-edify or restore these monuments of the past'.

Happily, many of the ruins that may have been referred to in these comments have now been taken into the care of the Office of Public Works and been well preserved and in some cases partially restored, such as Annaghdown, Claregalway, Cong, Moyne and Inchagoill. However this refers in greater measure to the larger and more imposing remains whereas the much smaller and earliest of remains are fast disappearing altogether. Many of these are hidden away on private lands and yet would be of enormous value to a wide variety of interests, both at home and from overseas, were they to be saved and preserved.

Whilst this book covers the early monastic sites around the Corrib Country, many of these sites have been overbuilt by medieval and later structures throughout the centuries. However, there still remain a large number of the original oratories and sites erected in the early centuries. These may have been architecturally humble yet still have special interest having evolved in almost complete independence of Roman traditions of building. The exact dating of some of this primitive building is often very difficult or impossible to determine. Moving inland from the coastal areas, timber, as well as stone, would have been the material normally used for several centuries and these primitive structures would date from the 5th, 6th and 7th centuries. However, through increasing contacts with the continent in the 6th–7th centuries onwards, the monks would also have become more acquainted with buildings in stone and mortar.

Early churches are very simple buildings of single chamber structure with no division into nave and chancel. Sometimes very small in size and measuring only ca. 3m x 2m internally in an east-west direction. The length is seldom greater than one and a half times the width which usually depicts an early date. It is interesting to note that the Brehon Law Tract specifically mentions dimensions of 15' x 10', i.e., one and a half. St MacDara's church on the island of that name has a plan ratio of 1.4 to 1. The general style of masonry is uncoursed rubble, many of the stones being quite large and mostly in the lower parts of the walls. In our limestone areas some of these larger stones were laid on edge and fitted together with great accuracy which was a distinct aspect of the very accomplished Irish masonry skills. The side walls are usually of no great height, only as little as 7' 0" in some cases, but the gable walls were relatively high because of the steep pitch needed if the roof was thatched or shingled.

Another characteristic is the inward sloping of the walls and doorways, known as the batter, which was very pronounced in the architecture of Egypt with its origins in the early buildings of Nile mud, with their broad-based walls sloping inwards to the sake of stability. These early monastic settlements were indeed very similar to the earliest monastic settlements of Syria and Egypt and through this ever spreading ascetic movement, these early monks sought out areas of isolation such as islands and inhospitable locations on our coastlines, even hilltops and remote valleys, which can be categorised in our word '*Dysert*' or desert (comes from *díseart*, a deserted place, a retreat or hermitage). One of the constant features of these early settlements was also the enclosure system which was an encircling rampart of earth or stone where the hermit would have been able to shut out all but the heavens from his sight and thoughts. A number of the sites in this book clearly depict some such enclosures and which I have been fortunate enough to have been able to photograph from the air.

So many of these early Irish saints had such powerful faith and ability to travel, to spread the message of Christianity wherever the Spirit led them and they proved to be the most intrepid travellers. Apart from St Brendan and his epic Voyage, they also travelled in the main to continental Europe where they set up so many monastic houses and where they are highly venerated to this day for the huge influence they brought. It is perhaps fitting to note that today all the Aer Lingus aircraft bear the names of these early saints.

Early monasticism in Ireland has a special uniqueness in the history of the Celtic or Gaelic church in that any organisation to do with finance, lands etc., was not governed by bishops but by the abbots of the monasteries. Sometimes the abbot of a monastery might also have been a bishop but otherwise a bishop's role was more of an itinerant and sacramental nature. As against other parts of the Roman world there were no cities in Ireland so the life and economy was wholly pastoral and based around local tribes or little kingdoms. So, this was largely an independent monastic movement up until the Synod of Rathbreasail in 1111, (*Ráth Bressail* – Ringfort of Bressail) when the first initiations of a diocesan system were introduced.

In any work describing the Corrib Country it must be acknowledged that probably the finest and most definitive research on its vast variety of antiquities and interests is to be found in Sir William Wilde's *Lough Corrib*, first published in 1867 and then wisely and generously reprinted in 2002 by Kevin Duffy of Headford. It is very closely followed by Richard Hayward's *The Corrib Country* published in 1968, which is a very worthy and comprehensive companion to Wilde's work. Constant reference to these two books in the reading of this simple guide will be of great benefit to the student and researcher.

The following will assist the reader's understanding of dating terminology:

Early Christian	ca. AD 400–1200
Medieval	1170–1350
Late Medieval	1350–1600
Romanesque Style	1130–1200
Transitional Style	1200–1250
Gothic Style	1250–1600

Early Christian churches were rectangular with a west doorway, a plain east window and projecting corbels or antae.

Medieval churches would have nave and chancel, i.e. enlarged oratories.

Late Medieval churches would be simple rectangular churches with doorways on one of the sidewalls, usually the south, and the frequent traces of either a loft, an extension or a subdivision at the west end which may have been living quarters for clergy.

Anthony Previté

Clonbur
Cong
Cross
Cornamona
Shrule
Inishmicatreer
Inchagoill
Lough Corrib
Maam Cross
Headford
Inchiquin
Oughterard
Moycullen
Claregalway
1
2
3
4
5
6
7
8
9
10
11
12
13
14
15
16
17
18
19
20
21
22
23
24
25
26
27
28
29
30
31

Lough Corrib's
Early Monastic Sites

1. Inchagoill
2. Currarevagh
3. Oughterard
4. Portacarron
5. Laghtgannon
6. Rosscahill
7. Boleyvaunaun
8. Killannin
9. Dovepark
10. Kilrainey
11. Moycullen
12. Killagoola
13. Clooniff
14. Claregalway
15. Annaghdown
16. Kilian Church
17. Kilcoona
18. Cloghanower
19. Cargin
20. Annaghkeen
21. Killursa
22. Ross Errilly
23. Donaghpatrick
24. Inchiquinn
25. Kinlough
26. Moyne
27. Inishmicatreer
28. Cross
29. Dowagh
30. Killarsagh
31. Cong

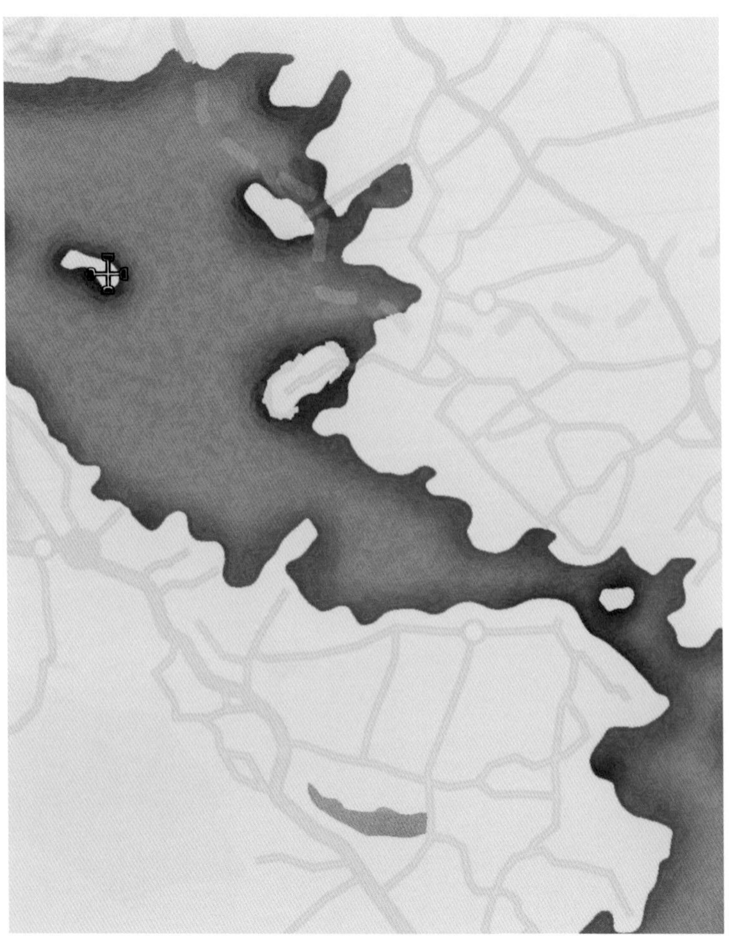

INCHAGOILL

N53°29 W009°18

Inis an Ghaill, the Island of the Foreigner, is possibly one of the most interesting islands of the Corrib, certainly having the most extensive and best preserved early Christian ecclesiastical remains. Although nothing is known of the early history of the monastic settlement, it contains two churches linked by a possibly ancient road. Associated with them are a graveyard, two cross-inscribed pillars, five cross slabs, and a small stone cross. There are also three bullauns, one now missing, and a holy well.

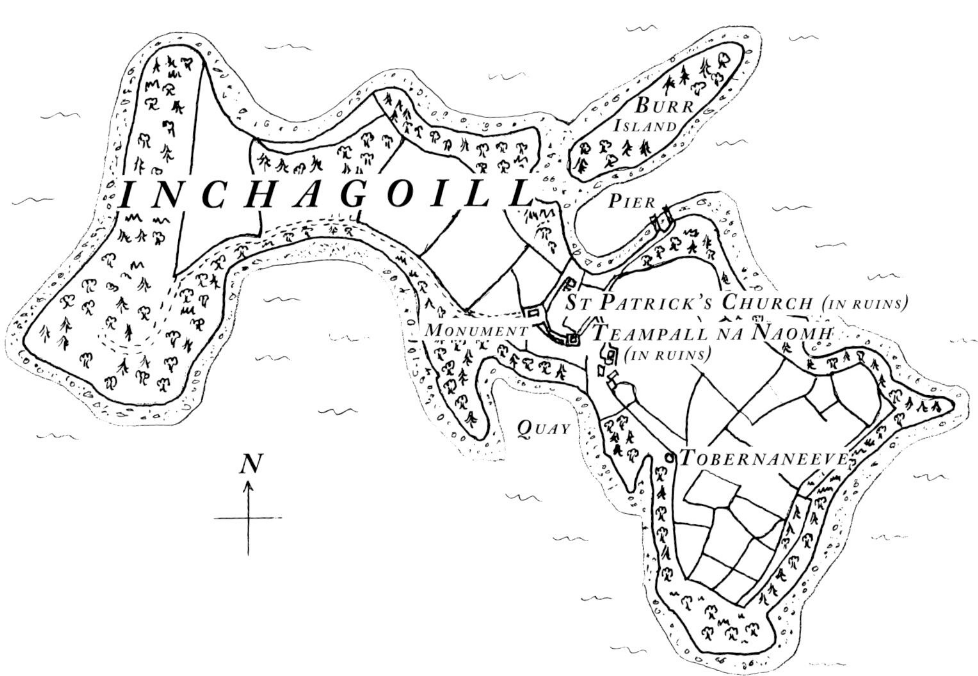

Long in shape, the island has a narrow belt across the centre and it is on a rise at this point that we find an extensive graveyard within the ecclesiastical enclosure. In the north east corner of this rectangular graveyard about mid-point along the island and ca. 150m south west of a landing place is the conserved Early Christian St Patrick's Church comprising a nave (E-W; 5.5m L x 3.65m W) with a later chancel (3.5m L x 2.55m W) at the east end. There is a trabeate door in the west wall and a robbed window in the east. One of the cross-inscribed pillars, famed for its 5th–6th century inscription to Luguaedon, stands in the south west corner of the graveyard. This monumental stone is a single, four-sided obelisk pillar of hard, greyish Silurian stone. The church is said to have been built by St Patrick and his nephew Lugna, who died on the island.

below: Church of St Patrick above left: View of east gable above right: West gable and door

The Stone of Luguaedon

This early cross slab (*see pictures above*) dedicated to Luguaedon is probably one of the most fascinating monuments to be found in the Corrib region. The inscription, said to be the oldest inscription in Europe done in roman letters apart from the catacombs in Rome, reads as 'LIE LUGUAEDON MACCI MENUCH, "The Stone of Luguaedon Son of Menuech". Professor Declan MacManus of Maynooth in his book *A Guide to Ogham* (1994) suggests that the usual reading of the name being LUGNEADON MACCI MENUECH, may come from an earlier form of Ogham transliterated into Latin and that 'MACCU' possibly denotes a relationship or kinship to a tribe, rather than a dynastic blood relationship. Another commentary (Ferguson & Stokes) says that if Menueh is a form of Liamain, which was the name of St Patrick's sister, then this may well be a memorial of Lugna, his nephew and who is reputed to have been St Patrick's navigator. If not, then a stranger of that name used the island as a retreat and may have been buried there, hence the name of the island: *Inis an Guill Craebhthaich* – The Island of the Devout Stranger.

There are other references in tradition to Lugna being a saint of Munster who died in 500–501 which may well have been on Inchagoill. St Ciarán's father is also said by some to be St Lugna, i.e. Ciarán Mac Lugna, and again, St Colman's (McO'Laoighse) is also said to be St Lugna and his grandfather was Eugene, the tribe name being *Mac Ua Loighse.*

Teampall na Naomh

About 75m south east of St Patrick's church are the walls of another church known as *Teampall na Naomh*, 'church of the saints' (*see picture below*), with nave and chancel (E-W; 10.15m L x 6.47m W). There is a beautiful Romanesque doorway in the west wall, a plain chancel arch, round-headed windows in east and south walls, and an external projecting corbel at the north-east corner of the chancel.

above: Chancel arch, altar and east window below left: South wall window, internal

above right: South wall window, external below left: East window below right: West door

The Romanesque Doorway

The term Romanesque, in its architectural application, may be defined, in a broad and general way, as comprising all those phases of European architecture which were based, more or less, upon Roman art, and were in vogue in Italy and north and west thereof from about 600 to 1200 AD. The style took on provincial differences throughout Europe and the Irish variant is the most original and truly national of Irish Architectural achievements. Few of the extant remains can be dated with any certainty but architectural history maintains the start of this decoration would have been in the later ten-hundreds until the mid eleven-hundreds.

Reconstructed at uncertain, but probable early date, is the doorway of this Inchagoill church (*see picture left*). It is now of three orders of pier and arch but there are indications that it was once of different and bolder design: the stones of the second order of piers once supported a soffit arch but have been turned through 90 degrees to face outwards, and the ribboned chevroned arch they now support was not designed for them. The outer arch springs from skewback stones which do not look original and its component voussoirs, each boldly carved with a human head, seem to belong to a different – perhaps larger – arch.

The door is built of a local sandstone (found near Cong village) full of small shells which have weathered away on the surface, leaving it pitted all over; a disfigurement which masks the design of the frieze-form capitals with their angel-masks which, while bearing a striking likeness to those of the Timahoe tower doorway, are more Scandinavian in character. The piers and outer projecting pilasters are shallowly wrought with colonnettes and fillets and rest on low bases of small relief, much worn, some of which have a zoomorphic interlace decoration. There is no doubt that the original doorway was bolder and deeper and had, as its second order, a soffit arch supported by the present pillars of the second order.

above: Cross slabs inside Teampall na Naomh below: Bullauns inside Teampall na Naomh

In the western corner of this church is one of the most remarkable pieces of carving on the island (*see picture opposite page*). It consists of a flat, irregularly shaped reddish stone, 2'2" H x 3'10" W, built into the masonry in this Cyclopean wall. Indented on its surface is the very ancient Greek or Byzantine cross, the base or skeleton of which is of the same type as that on the stone of St Brecain at the Seven Churches in *Inis Mór*, and on many Irish tombstones. A similar cross also appears on High Island off the coast of Connemara.

Outside the north east corner of the church is a stone structure of square masonry (*see picture opposite page*) believed to be the tomb of Muirgheas O'Nioc, Archbishop of Tuam, who died here in 1128.

above: Greek or Byzantine cross inside Teampall na Naomh
below: Structure which is believed to be the tomb of Muirgehas O'Nioc, Archbishop of Tuam

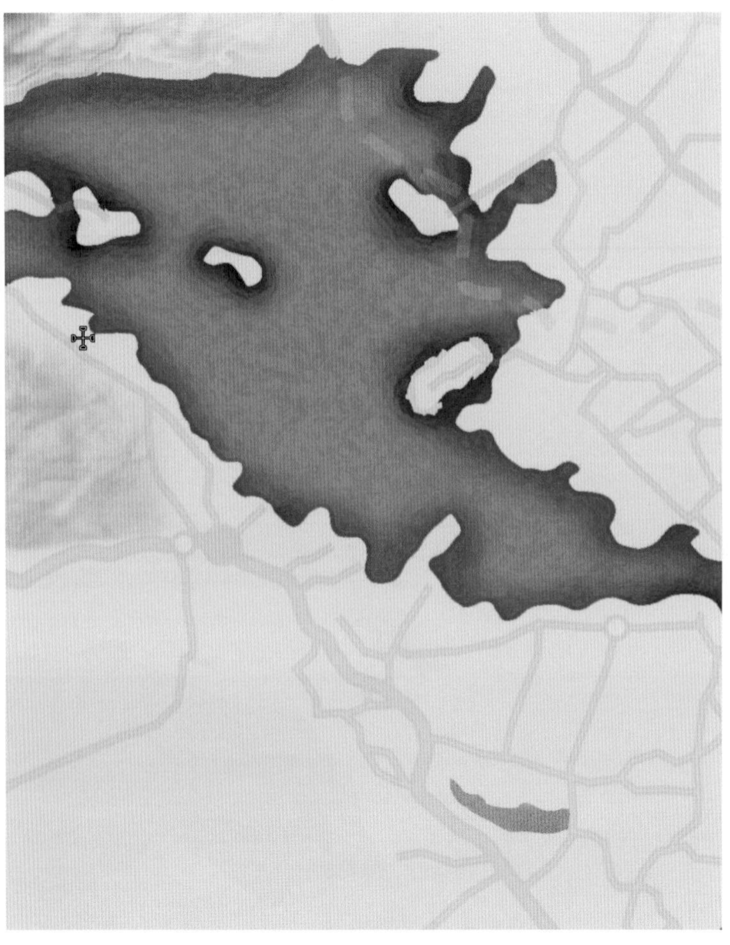

Currarevagh

N53°27' W009°21'

In the townland of Currarevagh (*An Currach Riabhach* – The Speckled Bog) is the burial ground indicated as Faughnakilla which is on a rise in a cleared area of what was otherwise forested land.

It is indicated on the first edition of the Ordnance Survey map as an unenclosed 'L' shaped area (ca. 25m x ca. 20m) but on the 2nd edition (1899) as a larger oval area. It is now enclosed by a concrete wall with the

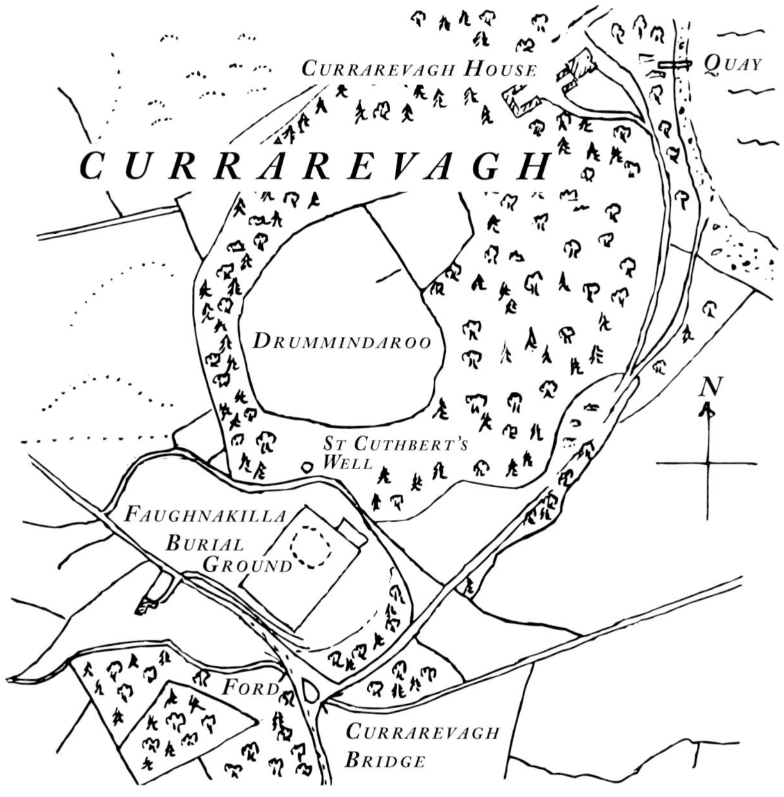

Graveyard showing ancient burial mound in centre

original burial area towards the centre which is the raised area and there is evidence of much stonework hidden under the long grass. A holy well lies ca. 45m to the north.

Burial section (Hodgson Family) adjacent to the north east of the walled in graveyard

There are a couple of possibilities with which to identify the dedication of this site from its very name, as Faughna can also mean Fachtna, Fhachtna or Fachanan. Of St Fachanan very little seems to be known with any certainty. However, his name is linked with Kilfenora in Co. Clare where he reputedly founded a monastery or church in the 6th century. There he is venerated as the first bishop of the See of Kilfenora, the administration of which is now entrusted to the Bishop of Galway.

Then there is St Fachtna, also called Fachtanan, who studied under St Ita and founded the monastery of Rosscarbery in Co. Cork before he died in 600 AD. This became the School of Ross, the centre from which the diocese of Ross developed, and flourished for about 300 years until the coming of the Normans to Ireland. His festival is held on August 13th.

The name Faughnakilla is also written in Irish as *Faiche na Cille* which could simply mean 'The Church Green' or 'The Burial Ground'.

It is interesting to note that the holy well just to the north of the site is not dedicated to Fachtna/Fachanan but to St Cuthbert. St Cuthbert of Lindisfarne (634-687) was an Anglo-Saxon monk and bishop in the kingdom of Northumbria, which at that time included the north east of England and the south east of Scotland. He is regarded as the patron saint of Northumbria and according to Irish Genealogies he was a second cousin of King Aldfrith of Northumbria. In 684 he was elected the sixth bishop of Lindisfarne in later succession to the third bishop, St Colman, who had gone on to establish his monastery on Inishbofin Island.

St Cuthbert's Well

Many churches, including Durham Cathedral, are named after him and some of the important locations in his life include Dunblane, Elgin, Iona, Kelso, Lindisfarne and Melrose. A strong follower of the ascetic practices in life, he also had a great love for animals and in Northumbria the Eider Duck is known as the Cuddy Duck, after St Cuthbert who protected them on the Farne Islands. His festival is celebrated on March 20th.

Oughterard

N53 25' W009 18'

Adjacent to the main road (N59) on a low ridge overlooking Lough Corrib to the north east in the townland of Lemonfield are the remains of a medieval church, 15.4m x 6m E-W, with a later south transept of 4.15m x 4.05m. There is a doorway in the south wall and opposing windows at the east end of the north and south walls, all robbed. The east gable contains a single-light ogee-headed window. A second doorway at the end of the south wall leads to the transept which is lit by a beautiful twin-light window, crowned by a circular ope, in the south wall. The large graveyard is mainly modern but its curving north wall may well reflect the line of an early ecclesiastical enclosure. The present ruins are now heavily covered with ivy and this will sadly cause further and considerable disintegration of the remaining stonework unless the ivy is cut or killed at the roots.

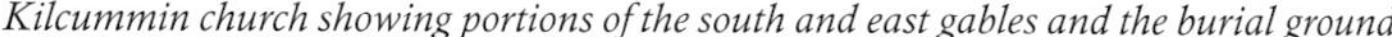

Kilcummin church showing portions of the south and east gables and the burial ground

Triple light window with circular ope – south gable elevation

This is possibly the site of St Cummin's Early Christian monastery, or at least one that he may have founded or is named after him. St Cummin was a monk from Iona and the remains of his original church are in fact to be found in the village of Kilcummin (*Cill Cuimín* – Cummin's Church) which is a at a beachhead on the northern coast of Co. Mayo. Those remains are dated to be earlier than the 8th century. His remains are buried there and the ancient headstone marks his grave.

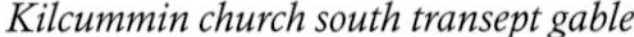

Kilcummin church south transept gable

Church of St Cummin at Kilcummin, North Mayo © John Musther

St Cummin's Well, Oughterard, near Kilcummin church, across main road

St Cummin, the First of Mayo, was the first cousin of St Tigernon of Errew and a contemporary of St Aodhan who ministered in Tirawley until his death in 562. St Cummin was about the same age as Aodhan and was born ca. 500 AD, 38 years after the death of St Patrick. Apparently there are another three men with the name of St Cummin, but the next one did not appear until 662 AD.

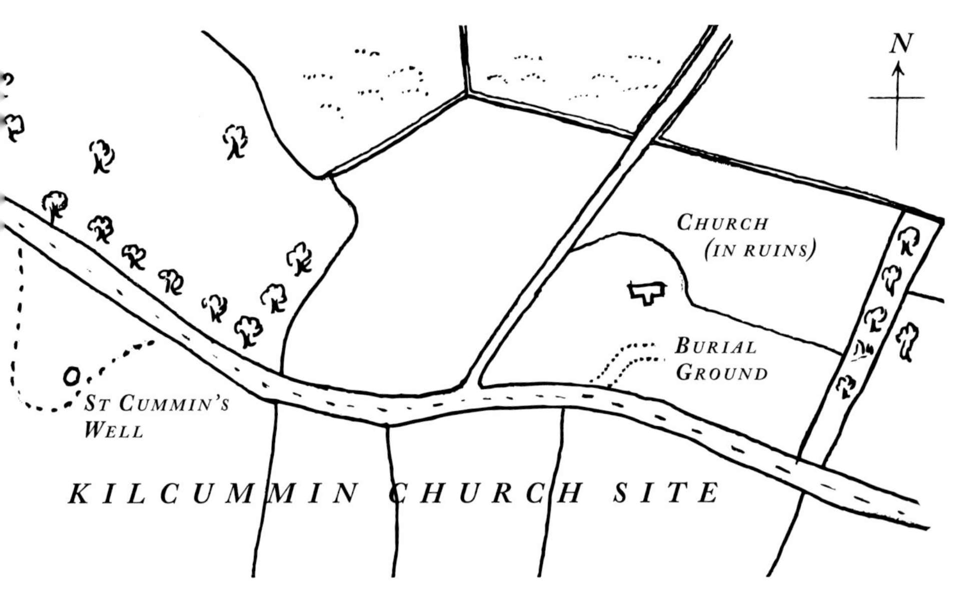

PORTACARRON

N53 26' W009 16'

Close to the west shore of Lough Corrib at Portacarron (*Port an Chairrín* – Harbour of the Little Stoney Place), is a large oval enclosure 94.6m E-W x 65.2. N-S, defined by an earth and stone bank, best preserved at the south, 2m W x 0.7m H, but disturbed elsewhere by farm buildings and modern walls. A small D shaped enclosure (20.5m x 11.2m), in the south half of the interior, contains the remains of a small, much ruined early Christian oratory (E-W, 6.25m L x 3m W). No architectural features are visible although there is still evidence of the trabeate door at the west end. The surrounding fallen stonework is of very regular and sound shape and must have been obtained from layered bedrock.

Enclosure with remains of oratory and small enclosure at the centre

The size of this enclosure and its walls would indicate that a substantial settlement existed here and an eventual archaeological investigation would possibly reveal foundations of early cells. Archaeologist Michael Gibbons suggests that some of the early buildings within the wider enclosure may well have been of timber and thatch construction.

These remains have been carefully fenced off and preserved by the property owner and would be an ideal project for research and restoration under the expert supervision of an archaeologist. Strangely enough, it does not appear to be known to which early saint this oratory might have been dedicated.

above left: Remains of oratory showing west door above right: Earthen enclosure
below: Aerial view of oratory ruins within small enclosure

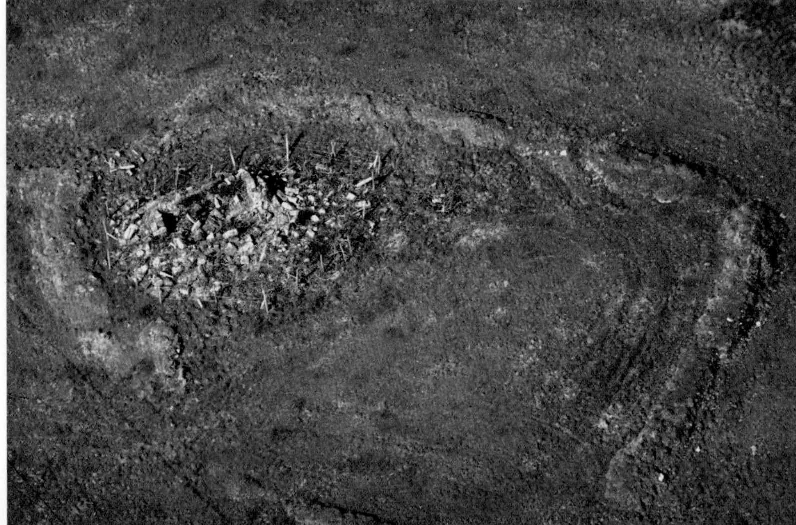

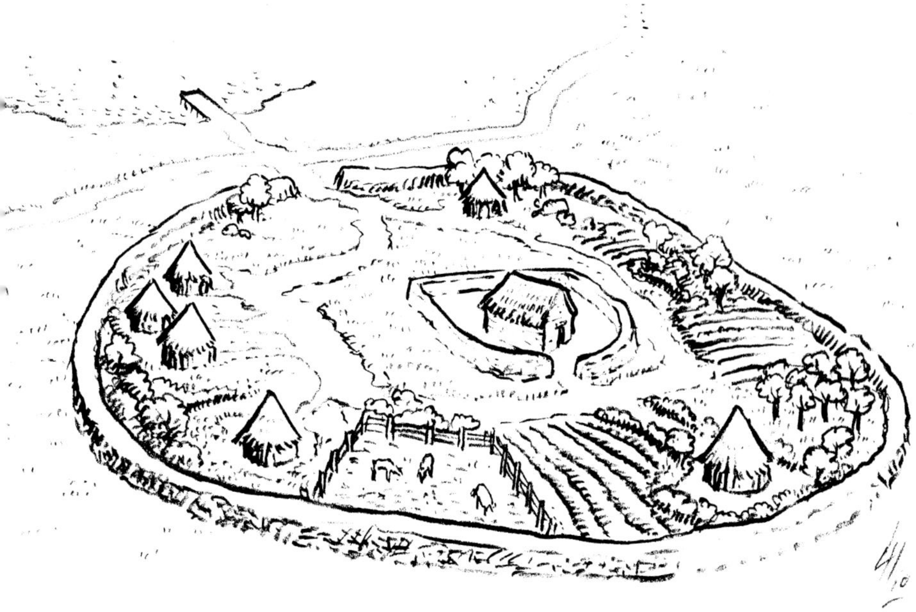

Artist's impression of original oratory (by Lol Hardiman)

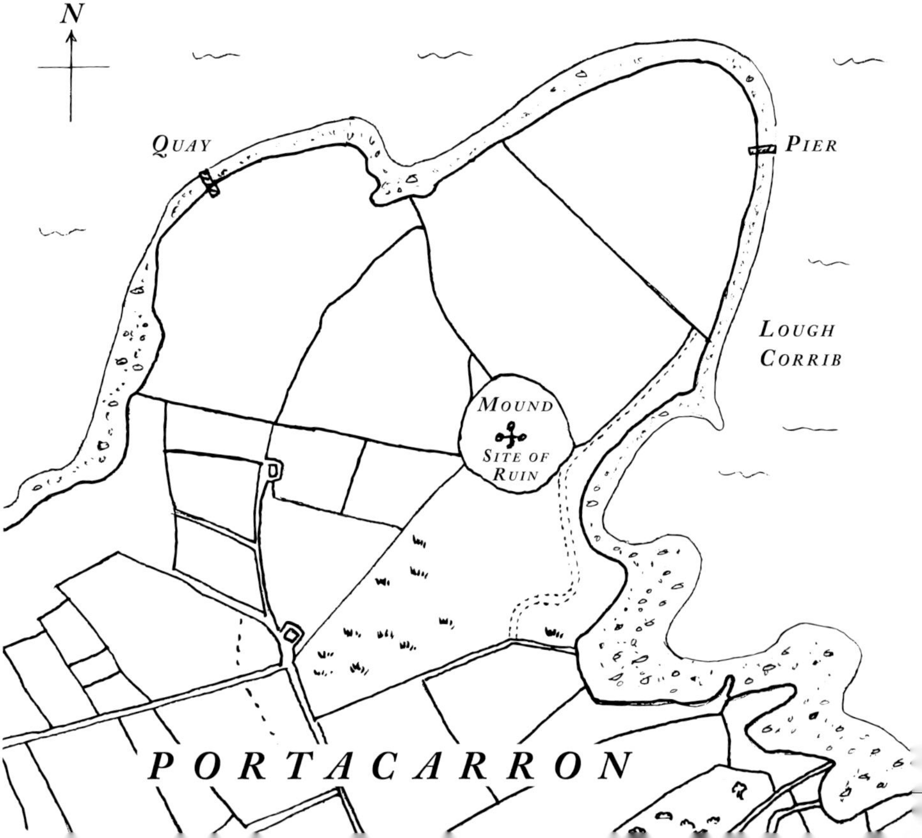

N

QUAY

PIER

LOUGH CORRIB

MOUND

SITE OF RUIN

PORTACARRON

above and below: Close-ups of remains
right page: Suggested plan and elevations based on foundation measurements

East Gable & Window *West Gable & Trabeate Door*

North Elevation

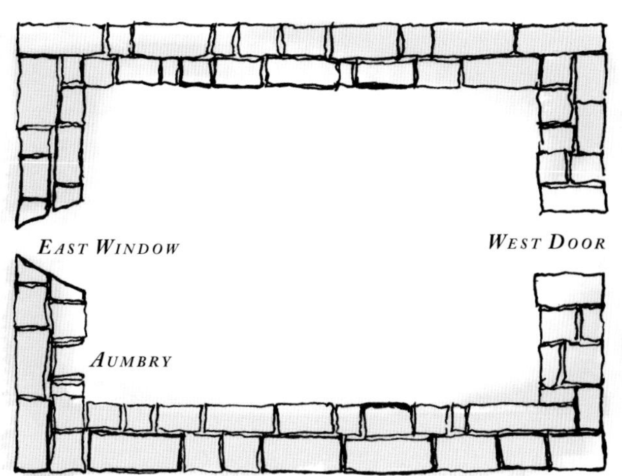

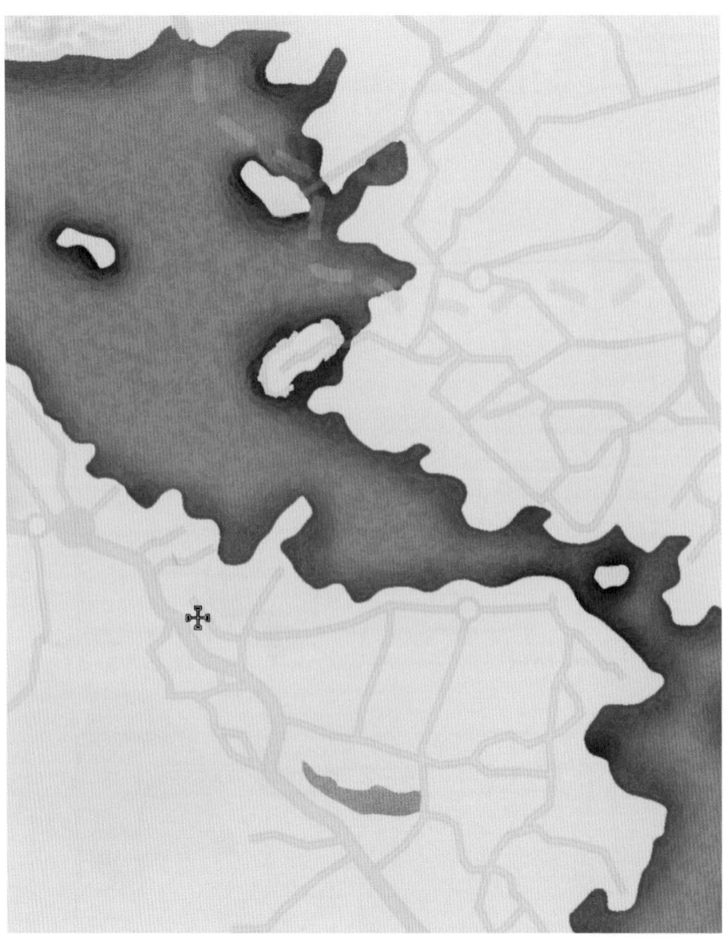

Laghtgannon

N53 24' W009 16'

In a graveyard adjacent to the main road (N59) at Laghtgannon (*Leacht Geanainn* – Gannon's Burial Stone) and a short distance to the east of Drimneen River are the very poorly preserved remains of a medieval church (E-W; 12m L x 5.6m W), indicated as Killaroon Church (*Cill á Rúin* –Church of the Secret), now known as the Church dedicated to St Croine. She was a virgin saint in the Carlow and Wicklow areas of the 6th century. Known as a recluse she was the daughter of Sedna, a descendant of Niall of the Nine Hostages (Celebrated on January 27th).

Remains of east gable

There is a possible doorway in the south wall and two short lengths of wall projecting ca. 2m beyond the west gable but do not seem to be bonded to it. This may possibly be either part of a priest's house or were buttresses to the wall. There do not appear to be any other remaining architectural features. The church and graveyard are now heavily wooded and cattle have trodden down most of the fallen stonework and the headstones beyond the east gable. A telephone pole also abuts this east gable!

above: Remains of south wall below: internal view of west gable

About 45m to the south west and in a field across the main road is a remarkable double bullaun.

Bullaun

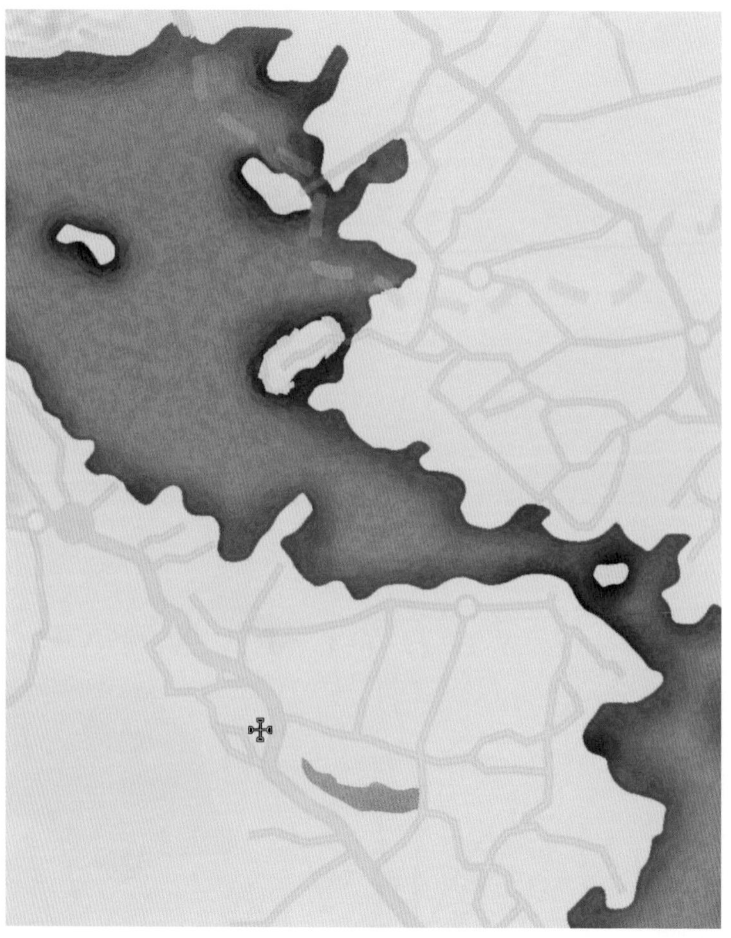

ROSSCAHILL

N53°23 W009°14

In an area of scrub and woodland to the north west of Ross Lake at *Ros Cathail* (Cathail's Wooded Headland) and immediately adjacent to the main road (N59) stand the remains of a much ruined Early Christian oratory (E-W; 4.6m L x 2.9m W). Indicated as St Brecan's Oratory, there still remains a good example of a round-headed window in the east gable. The west gable and parts of the north and south walls are destroyed. A small graveyard lies immediately to the west and a double bullaun ca. 50m to the south west.

Inside of west gable showing round-headed window

St Brecan or Brecain, can probably be equated with a comparatively obscure Clare saint of the same name whose dates are uncertain, but who may have been a patron of the royal dynasty of north Munster.

Windows in Early churches were few in number and small in size. Often the only one was in the east wall above the altar. They were very narrow, ca. 6", with inclined jambs and usually spanned at the head by a single stone in which the round head of the opening is wrought. Inwards from these narrow lights the jambs splay widely admitting the maximum of light offered by the small opening. This church still has a good example of such a window in the one entire wall which remains standing. In the past it seems that attempts were made to keep the site clear of trees, briars, etc., and it is hoped that similar efforts will be made to remove the present growth which threatens the survival of these remains.

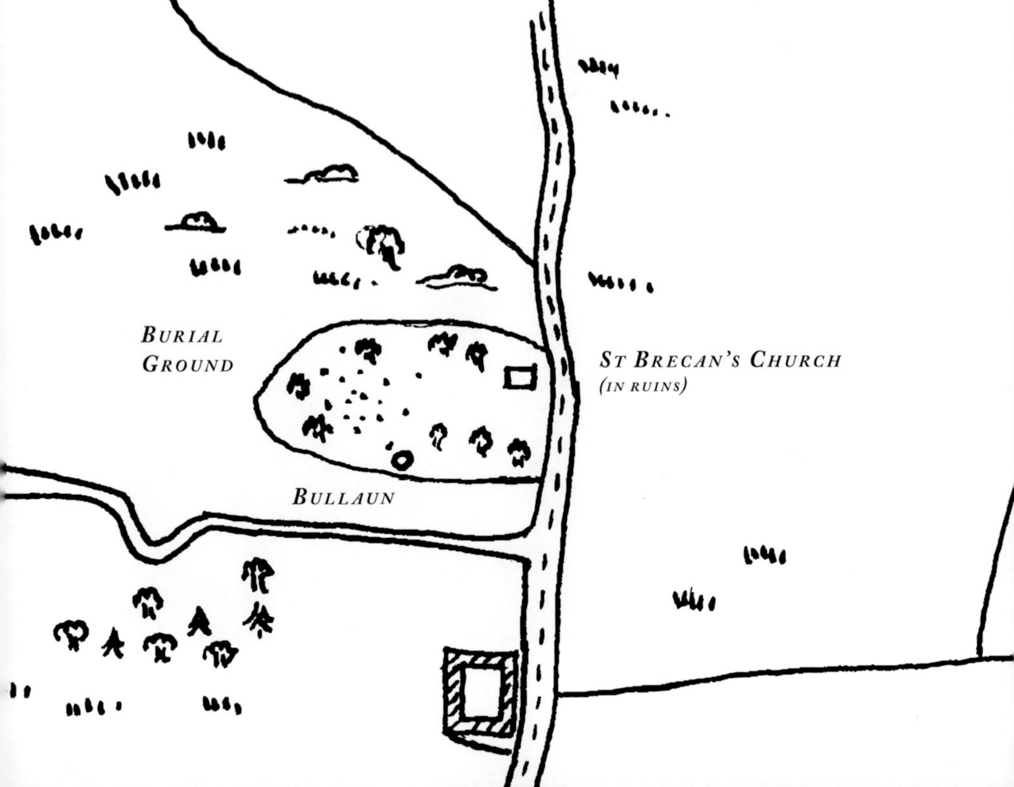

above: East gable from main road below: round-headed window

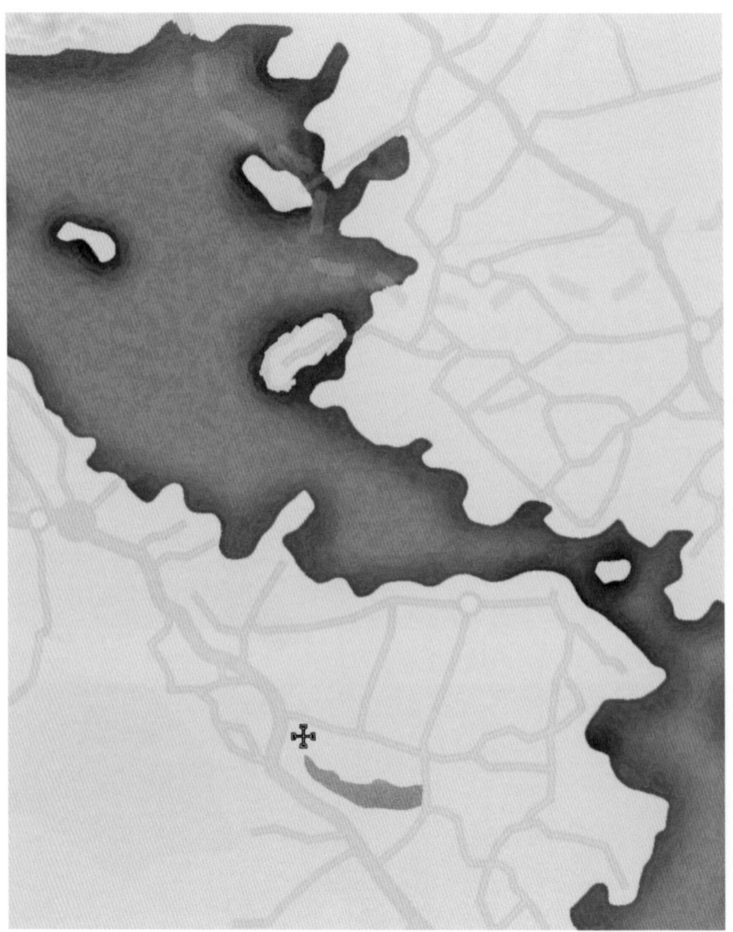

Boleyvaunaun

N53°23 W009°13

In undulating terrain in the townland of Boleyvaunaun *(Buaile Úi Bhánáin* – Summer Milking Pasture of the O'Bannons) and to the north of Ross Lake are the ruinous and ivy covered remains of an Early Christian oratory (E-W; 5.9m L x 3.65m W) indicated as *Teampall Beag na Naomh* – The Little Church of the Saints. This could refer to St Annin, whose Feast Day is celebrated on January 18th. Apart from a trabeate door in the west gable, it is otherwise featureless, although the north and south walls remain, but only the lower half of the east gable is standing. A bullaun lies ca. 100m to east-south-east.

North west view of oratory

The above illustration was accurately drawn ca. 1860 by Dr. R Willis of Oughterard when not yet covered in the usually considerable coating of ivy. The small doorway measured 5'6" H x 24" W at the base and 21" at the top which was the usual battered style. The stones were 2'3" deep and were the only ones of the building which had been 'dressed or rubbed'.

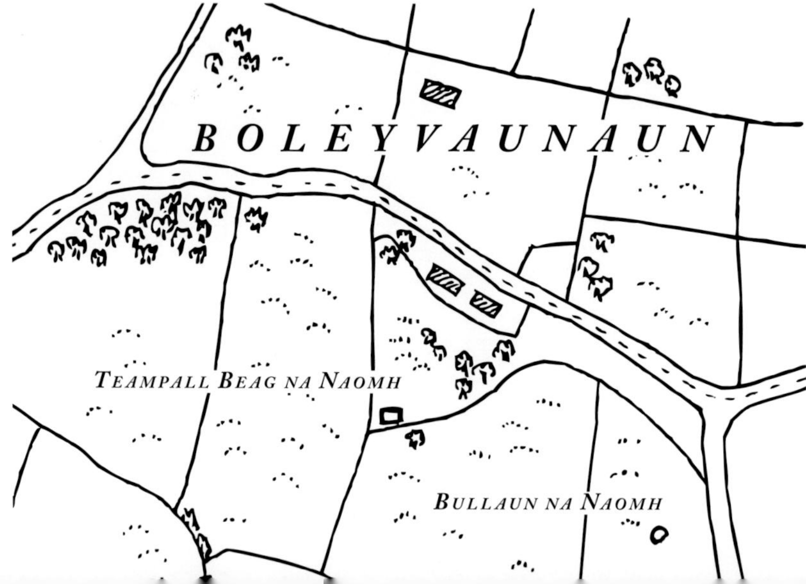

West gable (notice the accuracy of the stones with the drawing shown on page 50)

above: North west view
below: West gable showing trabeate door

KILLANNIN

N53°24 W009°13

In a graveyard on a slight ridge to the north of Ross Lake stand the remains of this poorly preserved medieval church (E-W; 13.9m L x 6.9m W) in a graveyard, dedicated to St Annin. There is a doorway in the south wall close to the south-west corner and a plain window in the east gable. Immediately to the south is a mortuary chapel containing the tomb of Major Thomas Poppleton dated 1848, a distinguished officer, esteemed by Napoleon, whom he guarded on St Helena. He is buried in this Martin family vault at St Annin's church as his wife, Violet Martin, was born at nearby Ross House, which he also owned for a period.

Remains of medieval church

The name of St Annin derives from *St Aithúin* which developes as *Ainfean* (meaning storm, violence or fury) who was a druidess at the time of St Patrick and of whom it has been said she would have been his lover had he not been so stuck on his celibate Christianity. Apparently she sought to combine druidism with Christianity but in any event she was eventually converted, baptised and then ironically taken in a Roman slave trade. Her feast day is celebrated on January 2nd.

Mortuary chapel adjacent to St Annin's church

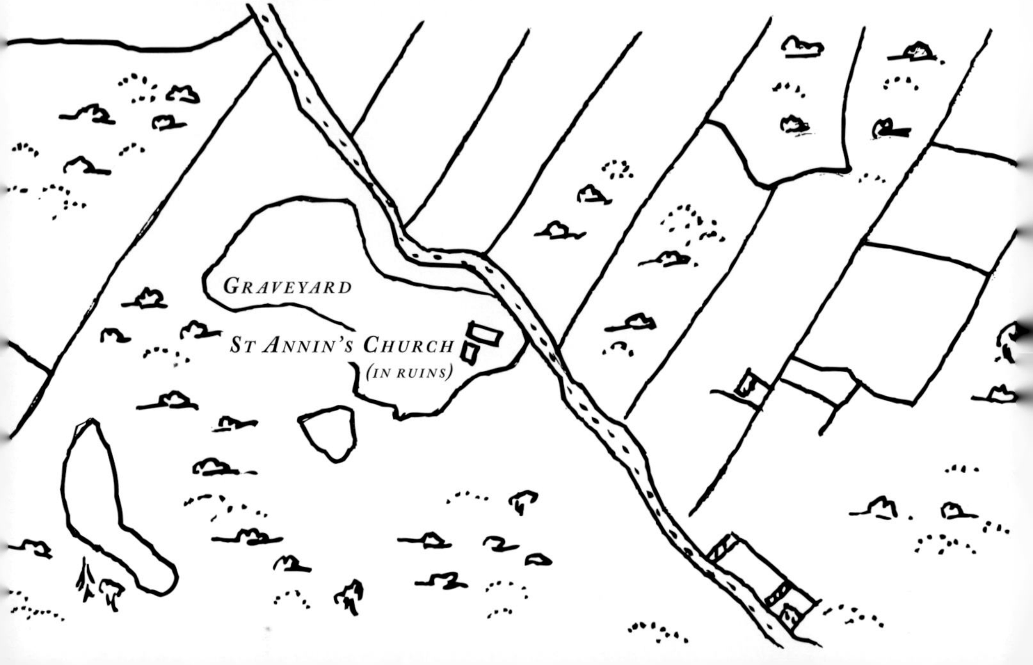

GRAVEYARD

ST ANNIN'S CHURCH

(IN RUINS)

Remains of enclosure wall

Pointed doorway of Mortuary chapel

East gable of church showing window and remains of altar below

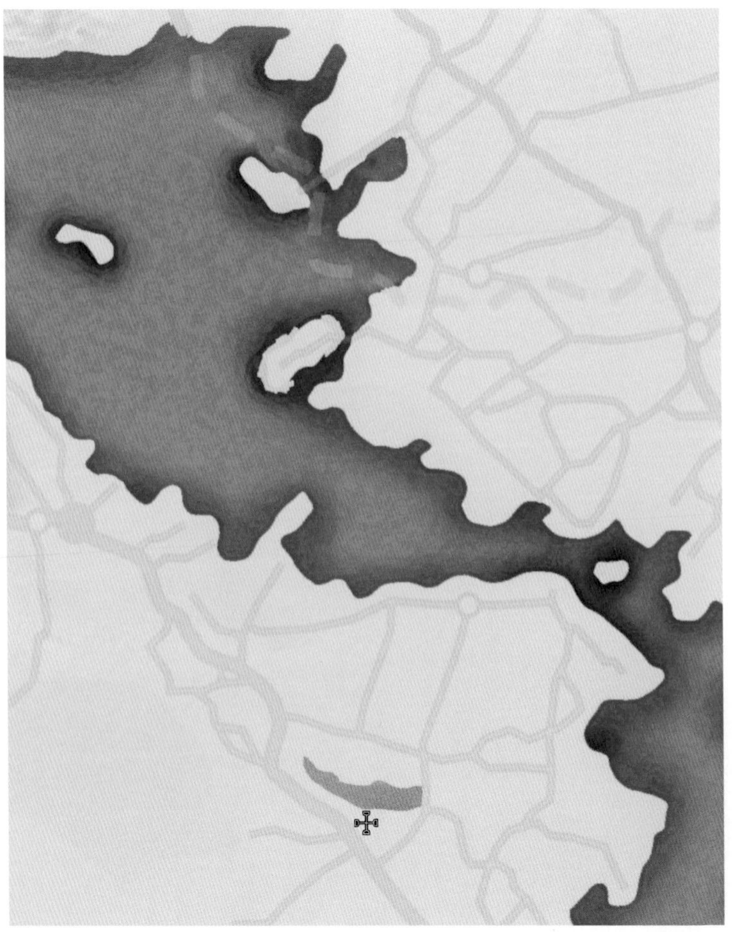

Dovepark

N53°23 W009°12

On a rise in undulating ground to the south of Ross Lake at Dovepark (*Páirc na gColm* – Field of the Doves) stand the remains of a very ruinous church (WNW-ESE; 11.46m L x 6.45 W), indicated as Kilcallin Church, probably medieval in date. No architectural features survive. There are faint traces of a curving scarp to south east, south and west of the church which may indicate the existence of an early ecclesiastical enclosure or ancient fort.

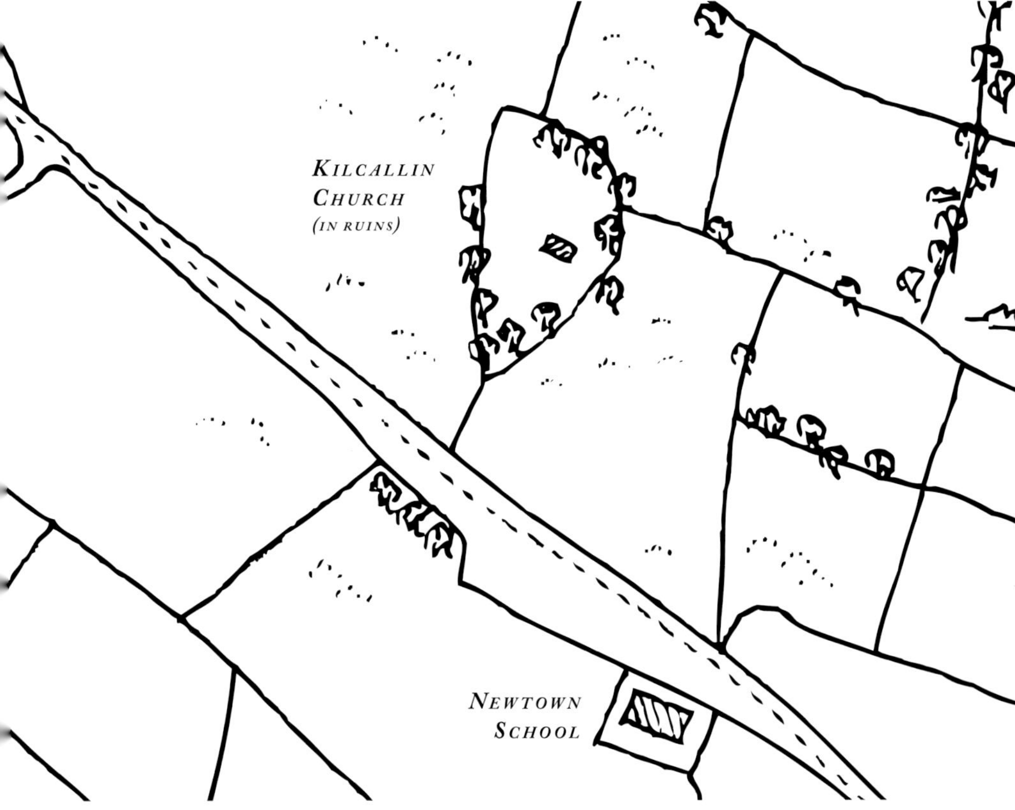

This little church may have been dedicated to St Caillin, one of the tribe of the *Conmaicne* which had split up between Connemara in the west and Leitrim/Cavan in the east. This eastern part of the tribe, which became known as the *Conmaicne Réin*, were apparently converted to Christianity by Saint Callan in 560 AD, who founded the monastery of Fenagh in South Leitrim. He would have been acquainted with many of the early Irish saints of which St Fintan was one and under whom he had studied as a young man. He spent a time evangelising in Scotland and is also said to have visited Rome. Upon his death his remains are said to have been buried in the walls of the ruins of Fenagh Abbey. His Feast Day is November 13th. (*See also Chapel Island, St Caillín, in A Guide to Connemara's Early Christian Sites.*)

Remaining north and west walls

above: East gable below: Interior

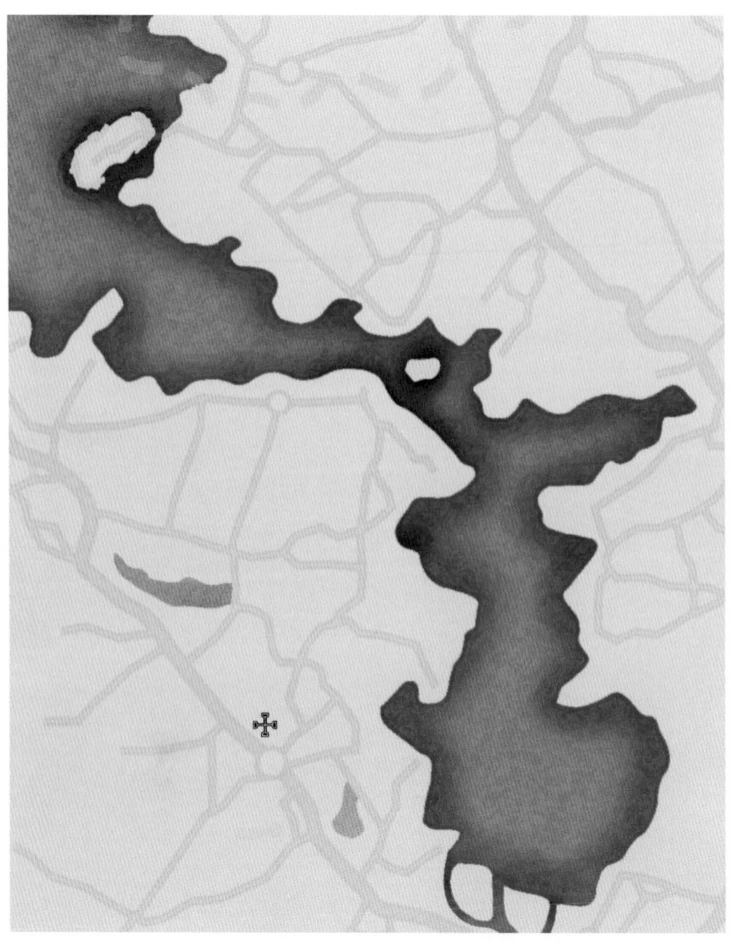

Kilrainey

N53°20 W009°10

In very dense scrubland near the centre of Moycullen village seem to be the remains of two circular enclosure foundations, each with a diameter of ca. 45m, now completely obliterated by the undergrowth. They are however clearly visible from the Google Earth maps taken in 2005. So far this has only been recorded in the Archaeological Inventory of Co. Galway as an unclassified earthwork or ringfort. However the very name seems to indicate a church. The name in Irish would seem to be *Cill a Raithneach or Raithnighe* which would mean the Church of or at the Rushes, although some tradition says it may have been the Church of the Rings. It could also be the Church of Enda's Fort, *Cill Ráth-Éinne. Riáin* or *Ráine* could also mean a Queen which was the name of the founder of a church in Donegal *(Cill Ráine).*

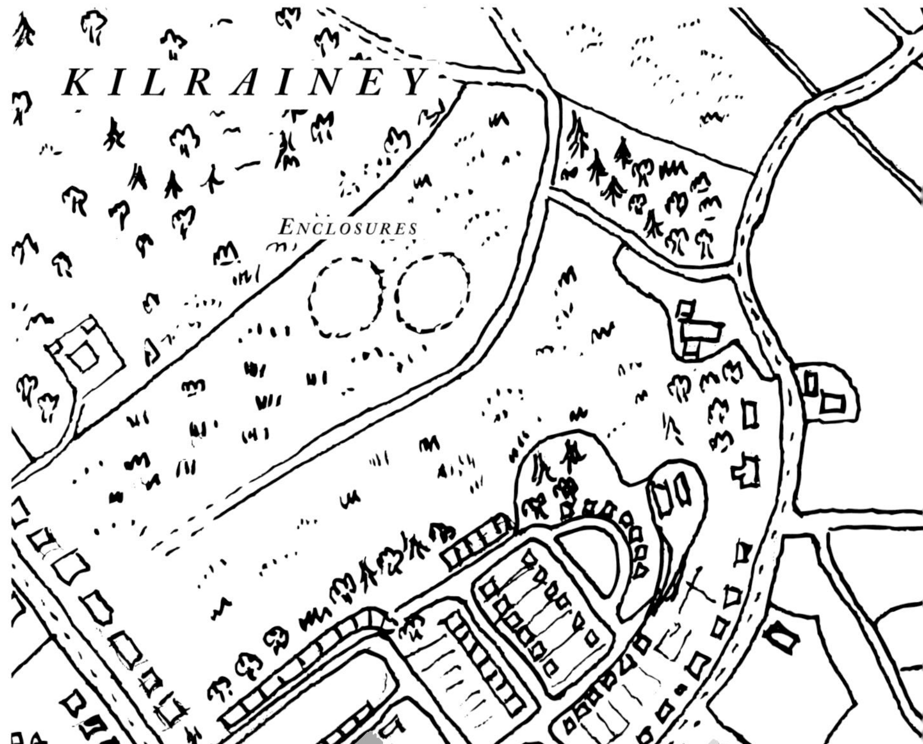

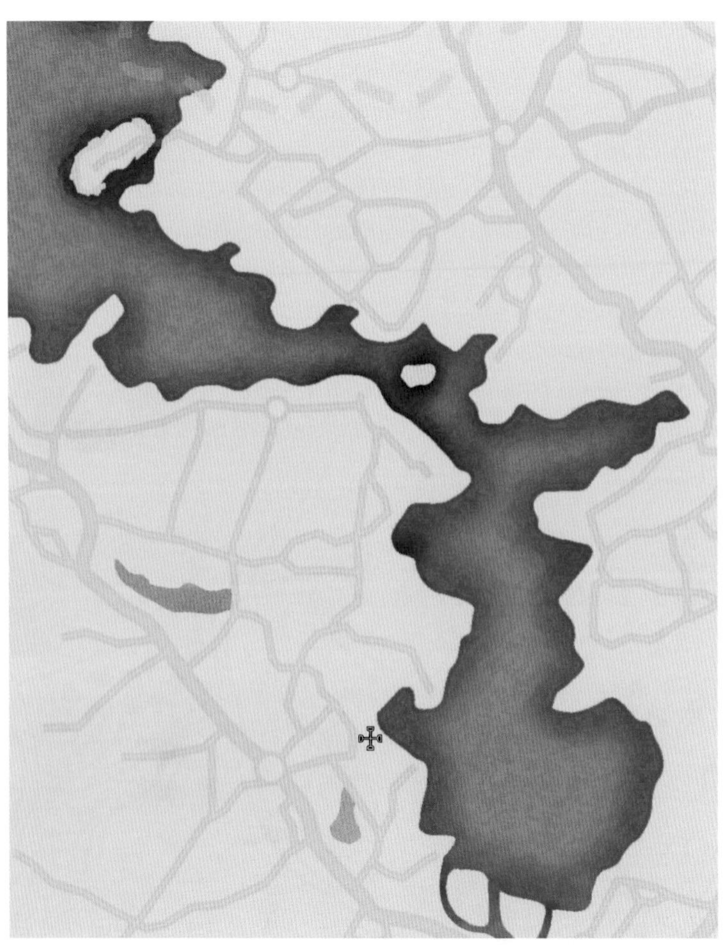

Moycullen

N53 20' W009 23'

In a graveyard ca. 300m west of what was formerly Moycullen Castle (*Maigh Cuilin* – Plain of Cullen) are the remains of a probable medieval church, densely overgrown and ruinous (E-W; 16m L x 6.6m W). There is a narrow single-light flat-headed window in the east gable but the north and south walls are almost destroyed. There remains a narrow single-light window in the remaining part of the north wall. The curving graveyard wall appears to be modern.

West wall of Moycullen Church, heavily overgrown with ivy

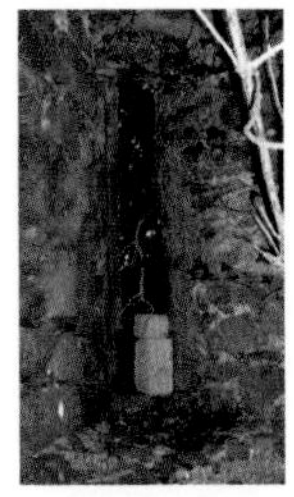

above left: East single-light window center: North single-light window right: Aumbry in north wall

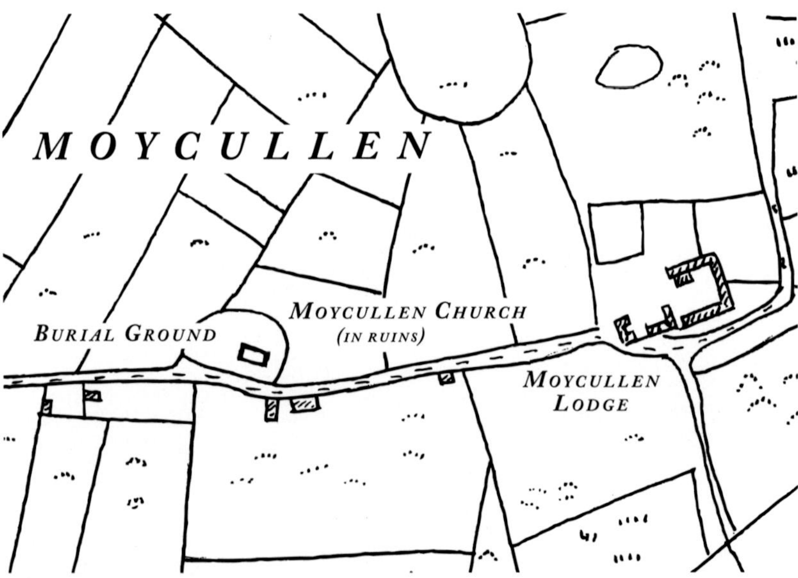

The nearby Moycullen Lodge/Castle was formerly the home of Roderick (Ruairi) O'Flaherty (1629–1718) who was born and lived here until 1649. He attended the Alexander Lynch School in Galway city, a school that was renowned for attracting scholars from all over Ireland.

Being Irish and Catholic, O'Flaherty lost all his wealth after the execution of King Charles 1st and fled to Sligo. Despite this he continued his studies in the Classics and History and wrote his first book in Latin. His greatest publication in English, *Chronological Description of West or Iar-Connaught*

Remaining east wall of Moycullen Castle, presently designated as 'Lodge'

was published after his death. This book was the first scientific account of fauna by an Irishman, other than that written by Augustin 1000 years earlier. The book provides information on the introduction of freshwater fish to Ireland and provides the first account of seabirds and marine life. It also includes an account of the first experimental study of animal behaviour recorded in Ireland. This study was made on the homing potential of salmon.

He was the last de jure Lord of Connaught, and the last recognised chief of the O'Flaherty clan. He is perhaps most often associated with his elaborate history of Ireland, *Ogygia*, published in 1685, *The Island of Calypso.* Drawing from numerous ancient documents, *Ogygia* traces Irish history back to the ages of mythology and legend, before the time of Christ. The book credits Milesius as the progenitor of the Goidelic people, an association which has since been called into question. Nonetheless, *Ogygia* is considered a definitive history of Ireland.

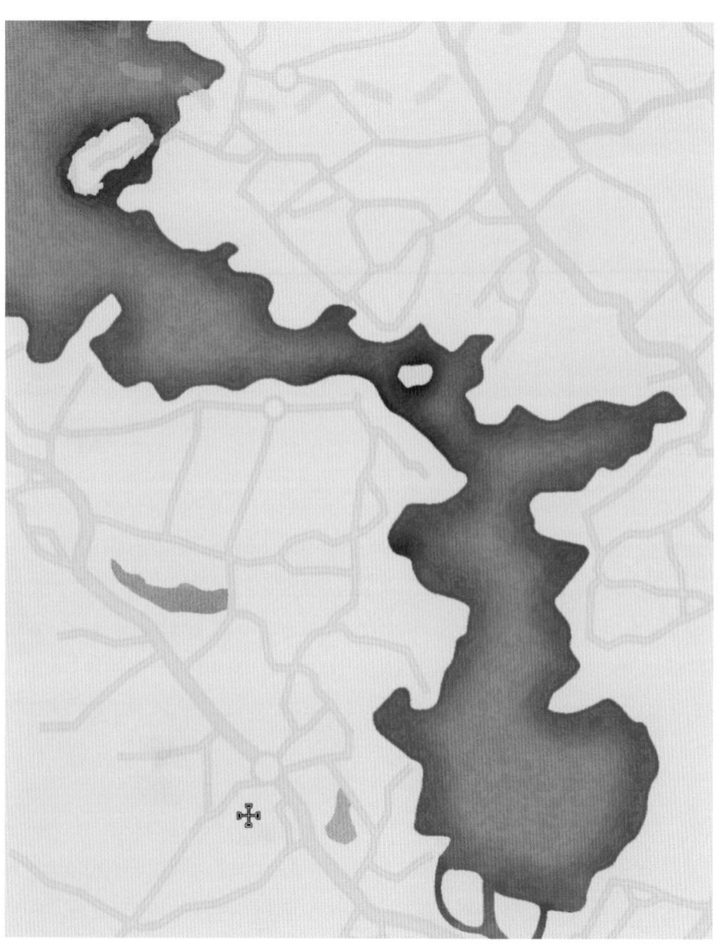

Killagoola

N53 19' W009 11'

On a level patch of ground on the south facing slopes of Killagoola Hill (*Cill Ogúla* – Ógul's Church) above and to the south of Moycullen village, is the much-ruined Early Christian Oratory (E-W 6m L x 4.1m W) dedicated to St Einne (*Teampall Éinne* – Enda's Church), with remains of a trabeate doorway in the west wall and foundations of what might have been a chancel visible at the east end (5.25m L x 3.8m W). However, this may well have been the original oratory and later converted into the chancel. Traces of a possibly modern rectangular building lie immediately to the north west. A low curving scarp traceable only to the north east of the oratory may be part of the early ecclesiastical enclosure. A holy well and a bullaun lie to the north west, and an extensive children's burial ground immediately to the south west.

Remains of church showing collapsed trabeate door in west gable

Holy well (Tobereany)

TOBEREANY

BULLAUN

BURIAL GROUND

TEAMPALL EANY

(IN RUINS)

KILLAGOOLA

Éinne is also the name for Enda who is the Patron Saint of *Inis Mór* and whose Feast Day is celebrated on March 21st. Enda was a prince, the son of Conall Derg of Ergall, Ulster. He was also a soldier who later became a monk, having been influenced by his sister, and studied with St Ninian in Galloway, Scotland. He founded his monastery on Inishmore (ca. 480 AD) on land donated by King Oengus of Cashel, his brother-in-law. This was apparently the first true monastery in Ireland and 10 other houses developed directly from it. Considered to be the father of Irish Monasticism, he was the spiritual leader of St Brendan, St Finian, St Columba, St Ciarán and St Jarlath of Tuam. Born in Meath he died in 530 AD and is buried at *Teaghlach Éinne* (Éinne's Household), *Inis Mór.*

Bullaun

Possible leacht

Remains of chancel at east end of church which may have been the original oratory

Children's burial ground (Cillin)

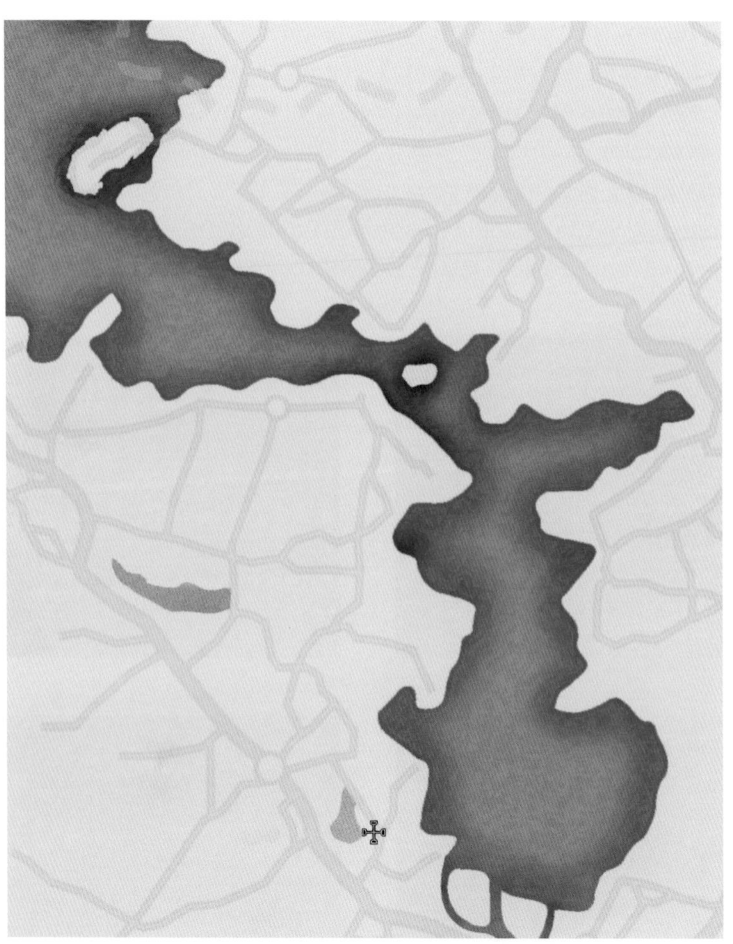

CLOONIFF

N53°19 W009°08

In the townland of Clooniff (*Cluain Duibh* – The Dark Meadow) and on level ground and within a small enclosure ca. 100m east of Ballyquirke Lough stands the much ruined Early Medieval nave and chancel church, *Teampall Beag*, (E-W; 10.7m L x 5m W) with a trabeate doorway in the west gable. Portions survive of a plain chancel arch of three orders. A bullaun lies 5m to the north west and there is a children's burial ground immediately to the south and east within the present enclosure.

Aerial view from east showing enclosure

The small enclosure contains quite a number of burials, but as seen from the photograph, the area is now heavily overgrown. In the not too distant past some attempts have obviously been made to preserve the walls of this oratory which is to be commended.

opposite page: West view of church showing west door and access to Ballyquirke Lake
above: Remains of chancel arch showing the three orders below: North west view

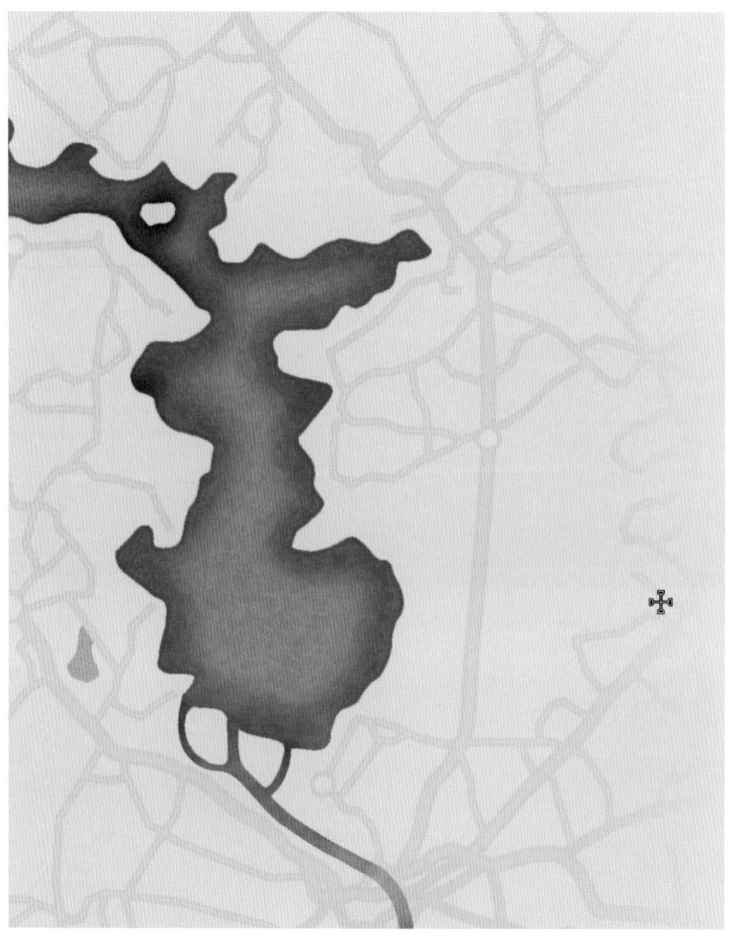

Claregalway

N53°20' W008°56'

Situated on the river Clare, which flows into Lough Corrib two miles to the west, stand the beautiful and imposing ruins of the 13th century Franciscan Abbey at *Baile Chláir* – Settlement of River Clare.

Claregalway Friary - photo courtesy of David P. Powell

Founded in 1252 by John de Cogan, a Norman knight who took possession of the area following the Norman conquest of Connacht, the abbey consists of a nave, choir, north aisle and transept, and is surmounted by its imposing 80' high tower of which parts remain in a good state of preservation and is a very significant landmark in the area.

View of cloister within the abbey ruins - photo courtesy of David P. Powell

The Franciscan community continued to live under the patronage of the de Cogan clan until the buildings and land were finally donated to them in 1327. The Franciscans remained there until the mid-16th century and the disruptions of the Reformation when it was ransacked by the forces of Lord Leonard Gray in 1536. In 1570, possession was granted by Elizabeth 1st to Sir Richard de Burgo and in 1589, the buildings were turned into a barracks under Sir Richard Bingham. By 1641, the Franciscans had reoccupied the abbey which by then was in very poor repair.

In 1731, Edward Synge, Church of Ireland archbishop of Tuam, recorded that 'there were at least three friars resident'. Church records indicate that the community numbered about 220 in 1766 but had dwindled to ca. 150 by 1782, and by 1838 it was down to only two members. They then departed for a larger community in Galway in November 1847. In 1892 a Lord Clanmorris donated the property to the Commissioners of Public Works by which organisation it is now maintained to this day.

The abbey consists of a nave and chancel of 13th–15th century date, with a later north aisle, three-storey tower and north transept probably of 15th

Remains of the friary's living quarters - photo by Andreas F. Borchert (license CC-BY-SA-3.0)
below: Inside view of the friary's living quarters

century. Immediately to the south are the cloister garth and large sections of the domestic ranges. Further south are the remains of the 'garderobes' and a water mill. Both in the graveyard and within the walls of the abbey can be found several tombstones bearing occupational symbols.

left page: Claregalway Friary tower - photo by Andreas F. Borchert (license CC-BY-SA-3.0)
above left: East window through tower arch right: Sedilia/Piscina

On the southern side of the River Clare and directly south of the present Friary are more but very ruinous ecclesiastical remains consisting of what looks like a rectangular church with only the remains of a north and south wall. There are scant remains of a pointed doorway in the north wall and an aumbry in the south wall. There are many burials within these walls and a great deal of unclassified and loose stonework outside the walls. These remains are marked on an archaeological map as an abbey and graveyard but no other information is given.

Internal view of ecclesiastical remains

above: Remains of doorway

above left: Burial stone above right: Aumbry below: External view of north wall

above: Curved entrance wall with Friary in background
below: View from east across what is listed as 'graveyard'

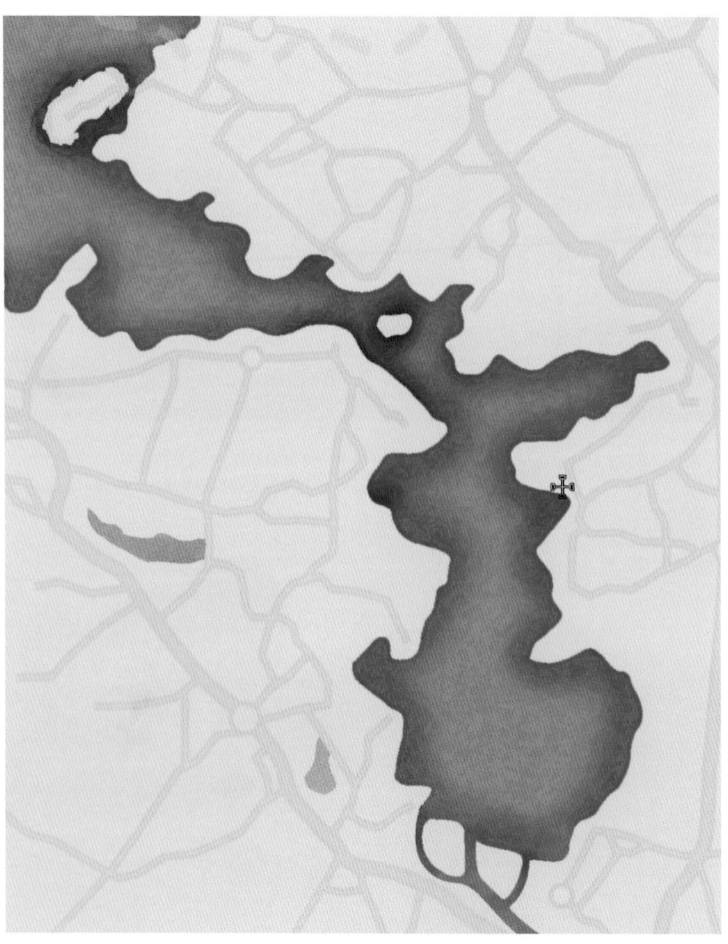

Annaghdown

N53°23 W009°04

According to the Book of Ballymote (compiled ca. 1390 from several other sources), Aodh, son of Tirmacarna, King of Connacht, bestowed Annaghdown on God and Brendan and here he brought his sister Briga, who was a canoness of the Augustinian Order, to found herself a nunnery, the remains of which, probably the oldest at Annaghdown, now stand to

Monastic and later remains of Briga's nunnery

the north of the present group of ruined buildings. So, this early monastic settlement (*Eanach Dhúin* – Marsh of the Fort) is said to have been founded by either St Brendan the Navigator or St Ciaran of Clonmacnoise. St Brendan is referred to under the chapter on Inchiquinn Island (*see page 125*) where he had also founded a monastic settlement so he was definitely very familiar with the area around Lough Corrib. The Annaghdown settlement was most likely to have been the foundation for nuns and of which his sister Briga was to become the abbess.

Nunnery windows

South door of nunnery chapel

It is recorded that following his return from his epic voyaging and in his fifties, Brendan still continued his missionary work throughout the West of Ireland, yet died in 577 in his sister's care in Annaghdown after a long and fruitful life at the age of 93. According to his wishes he was buried at Clonfert, the famous monastic centre he had founded in 563.

It is interesting to note that the Sicilian town of Bronte, as so often elsewhere, also has a church dedicated to St Brendan, whose name in the local dialect is *San Brandanu*. Since 1574 the present *Chiesa di San Brandano* replaces an earlier chapel of that name which had existed in the same location.

The claim that St Ciaran was the original founder of this Annaghdown settlement occurs in *Comainmniguid Noem nErenn* composed ca. 800 and contains a reference to *Ciarán Enaigh Dhúin* – Ciarán of Annaghdown. This and place name evidence may well indicate an association with Ciarán of Clonmacnoise who may certainly have spent time here.

East gable and window of 15th century C of I Cathedral

15th century Cathedral south wall

Romanesque east window, robbed from neighbouring priory

This 12th century Romanesque window opening (*above right*) measures 8' H externally and 12' H internally. It is deeply splayed internally with a rich variety of delicacy and design in its splayed stone carvings and decoration. On each side of the half round moulding where it joins the gable wall, there is a line of decorated chevrons between which are featured 66 different floral ornaments.

The ruined priory church in the background, dedicated to St Mary de Portu Patrum, with a cloister to the south and the remains of the priory buildings in the foreground.

right: The ruined east gable of priory chapel showing the empty gap where the fine Romanesque window had been removed and installed in the east gable of the neighbouring cathedral

below: Priory door showing built-in and highly carved pilasters

Annaghdown priory

Panoramic view of Annaghdown priory - photo © www.johnsmyth.ie

Annaghdown was established as a diocese in the 12th century with the cathedral having a dean, a chapter, and four vicars choral. Between 1253 and 1306, the bishopric was united to the archbishopric of Tuam, although in this period there were two bishops.

During the Reformation, there were two bishoprics; one of the Church of Ireland and the other of the Roman Catholic Church. They were re-united under Queen Mary 1st. After 1555, Annaghdown was held by the archbishops of Tuam and the union of the two was finally decreed on October 17th, 1580.

In 1970, the Roman Catholic Church revived the title as the Titular Bishop of *Eanach Dhúin*. There have been four such bishops appointed, i.e. Bishop of Westminster, England, bishop of Christchurch, New Zealand, the apostolic nuncio to Burundi and the present incumbent since 2006 is the auxiliary bishop of New York, Octavio Cisneros.

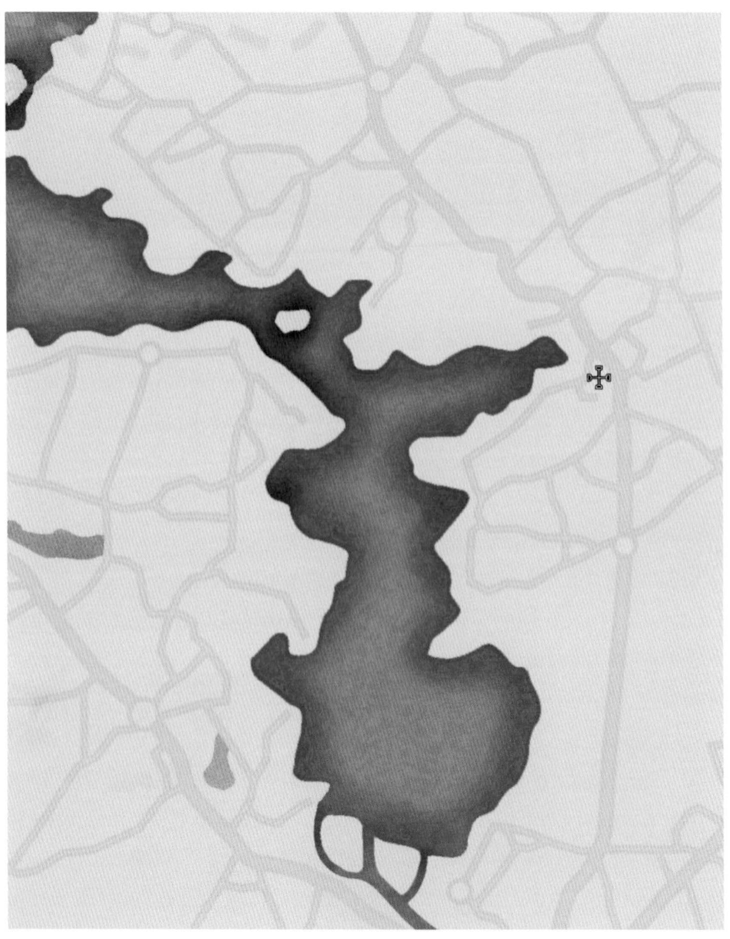

Kilian Church

N53°24 W009°01

Situated on a rise just to the left of the main Galway to Headford road and 60 yards down a by-road towards Annaghdown in the townland of Grange, stand the ruins of an ancient church in pasture land but heavily surrounded by trees, the boundary of which is the original circular enclosure wall. No architectural features remain of this church except occasional pieces of the wall foundations measuring approximately 60' x 27' externally.

Remains of south wall

This little church was dedicated to St Kilian who was born in Mullagh, Co. Cavan in 640 AD, and is the patron saint of the parish of Tuosist, near Kenmare in Co. Kerry where he is believed to have resided before he travelled to Germany. This journey he undertook via Rome in 686,

above: Another fragment of south wall below: Burials at east end of remains

together with eleven companions, after he was consecrated bishop. He had received permission from Pope Conon to evangelise in Baden and Bavaria (Franconia). Apparently he was successful in this endeavour together with two followers, Frs Colman and Totnan, until he converted Gosbert, Duke of Würzburg, who had married his brother's widow, Geilana. According to legend, whilst Gosbert was away on a military expedition, Geilana is reputed to have had the three missionaries beheaded when she found out that Gosbert was going to leave her after Kilian had told him that such a marriage was forbidden by the Church.

The elevation of the relics of these three martyrs was performed by Burchard, the first bishop of Würzburg. Their skulls, inlaid with precious stones, have been preserved to this day and are paraded in a glass case and put on display in Würzburg Cathedral on St Kilian's Day, celebrated on July 8th. The Cathedral is also dedicated to St Kilian. The statues of these three saints, along with many others, line the famous Saint's Bridge across the River Main. St Kilian is also the patron saint of wine makers and sufferers of rheumatism. The *Kiliani-Volkfest* (two weeks in July) is the main civil and religious festival in the region around Würzburg.

above: St Kilian and Fortress Marienberg - photo by Christian Horvat (license CC-BY-SA-3.0)

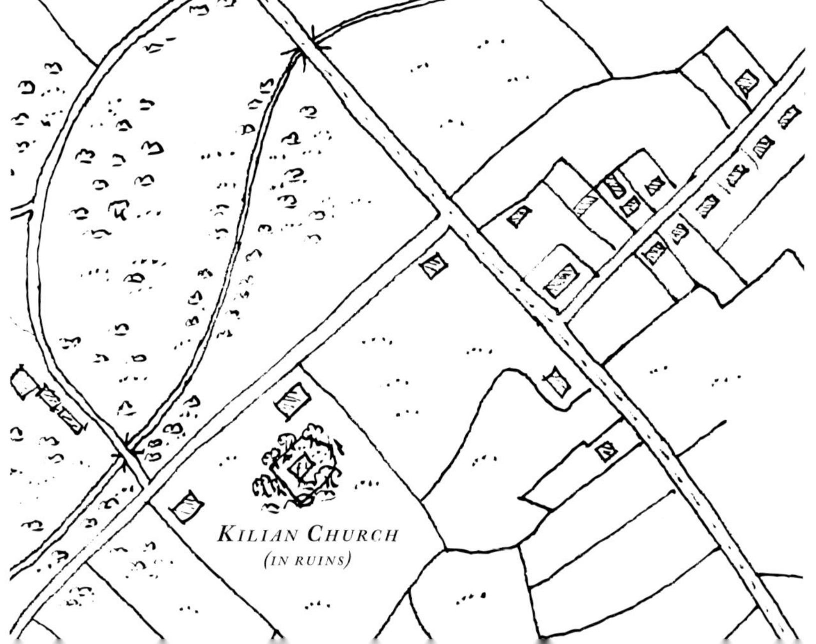

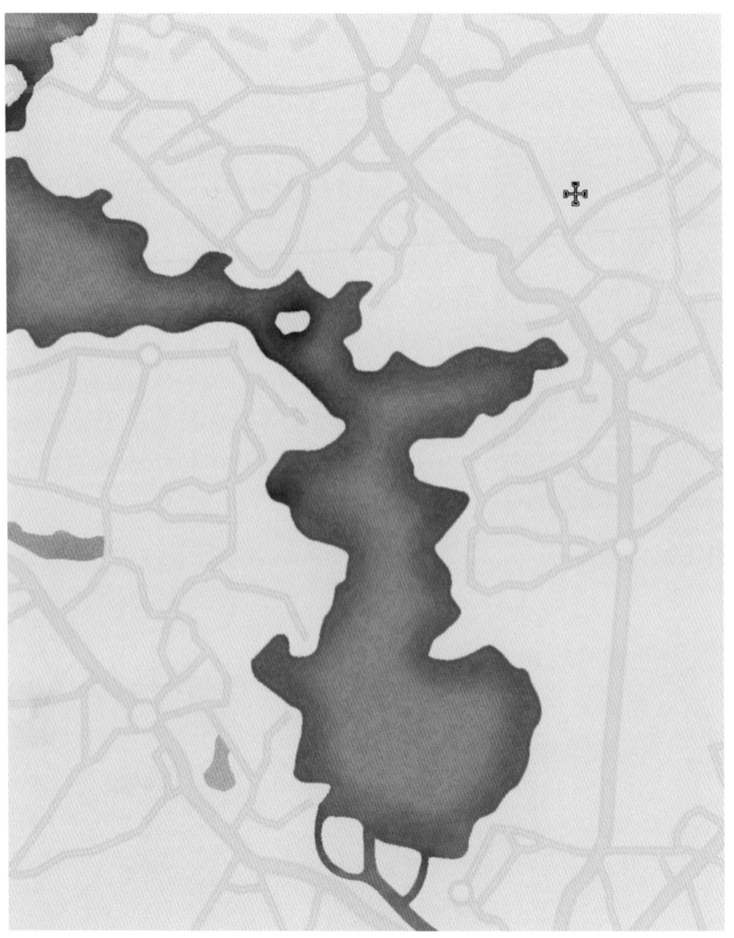

Kilcoona

N53°26 W009°01

About 2 miles south east of Cloghanower on the road towards Galway and then about a mile to the left, stands what remains of a 12th century church on the earlier site of a monastery, Kilcoona (*Cill Chuanna* – The Noble Church), founded by St Cuanna at the beginning of the 7th century. These ruins indicating a church 66'5" L x 24' W with part of the gables still standing, are in such a fragmentary state that no carved or worked stone is visible which might yield indications as to any architectural style of the settlement.

Remains of tower base and south wall of church

However, to the south west of the building remains the stump of a Round Tower (built, according to the annalists, ca. 1258), which shows excellent craftsmanship in the laying of the carefully dressed stones in regular courses cut into one another in the manner of ancient cyclopean masonry. No sign of a doorway remains as this may have been placed at a greater height than the existing walls which stand ca. 8' high with a girth of ca. 51'. They are now filled with solid matter and like many other stone remains are also covered in ivy.

Remains of Round Tower

St Cuanna (hound or wolf), born ca. 500 AD, was possibly the great great grandson of Niall of the Nine Hostages, the Great King of Ireland. His mother was Meda or Finneda, daughter of Fingen, a nobleman in the western district of Munster, and whose origin was derived from the tribe and territory of *Corca Dhuibhne*. She is said to have been the mother of four distinguished men, the first of whom, Carthac, son of Findall, was Abbot of Rathan in Meath. The second, St Cuanna, whose festival and natal day is February 4th, became Abbot of this monastery known as *Cill Chuanna*. He is said to have died about the year 650 AD, and is reputed to have written a chronicle of his own time, or *Annals of Ireland*, up to 628 AD. He had seemingly gathered around his settlement a large number of learned Christians when the whole of this region from Claregalway to Cong was greatly populated with men of learning, piety and art.

above: Window and door in remains of south wall below: Part of ecclesiastical enclosure wall

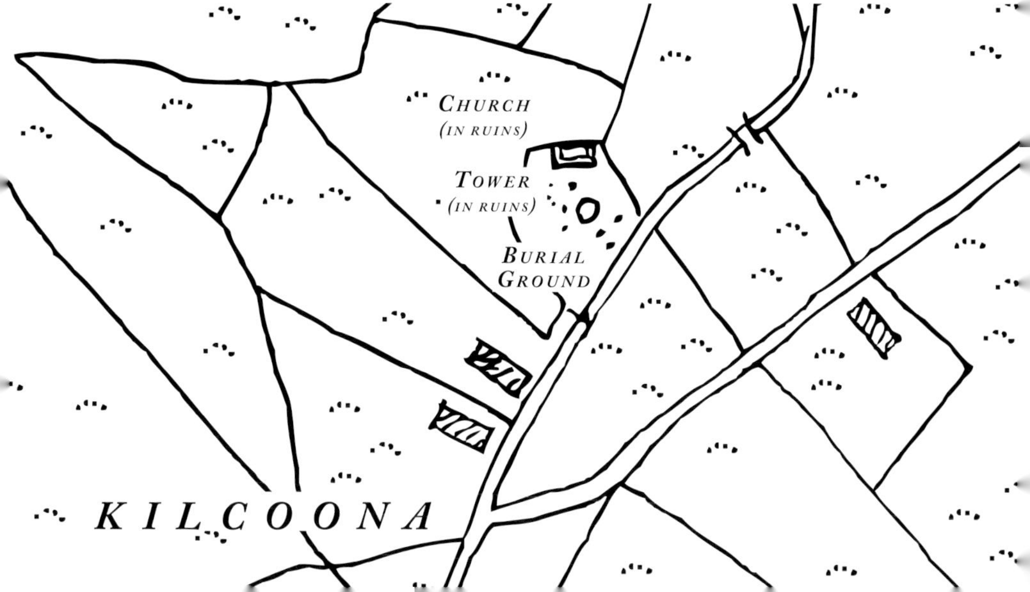

CHURCH
(IN RUINS)

TOWER
(IN RUINS)

BURIAL
GROUND

KILCOONA

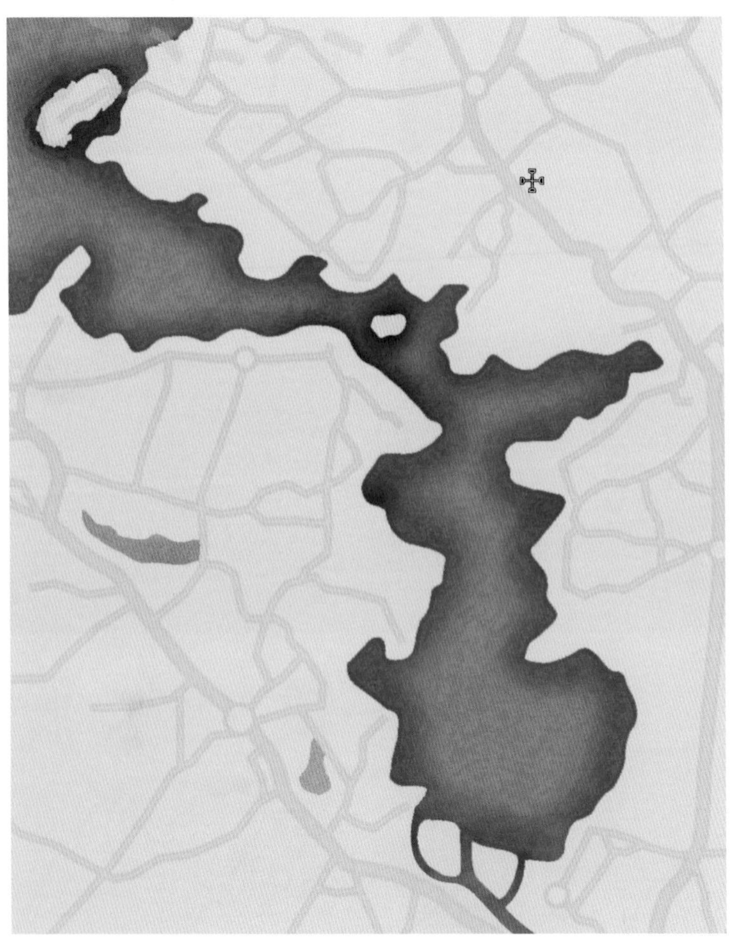

Cloghanower

N53°26 W009°05

On a small height a short distance to the north of the main Galway to Headford road stand the remains of an early monastic oratory of *Cloch an Uabhair* (the stone of pride) consisting of three partial walls still standing and a small window in the north wall. It is surrounded by a well-kept burial ground but heavily overgrown with ivy.

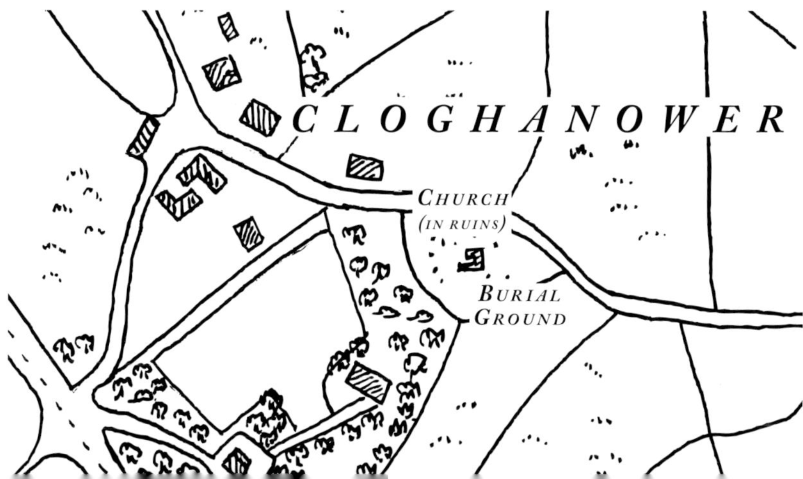

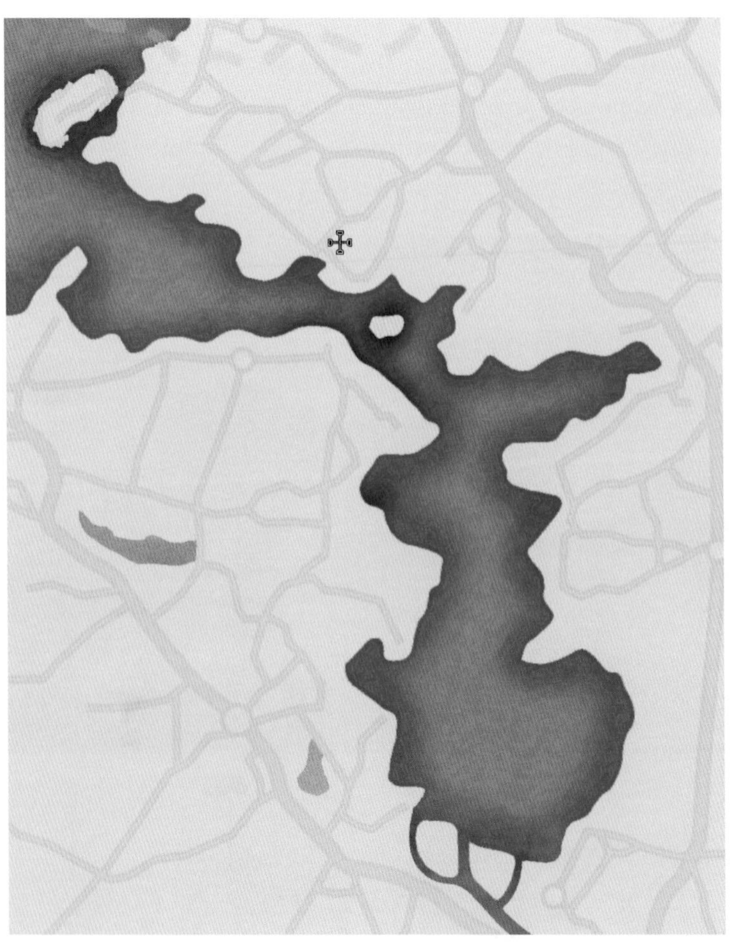

N53°26 W009°09

The ruined remains of Cargin Church are located approximately 4km south west of Headford town and accessed from a minor road leading south west to Lough Corrib. Its name is derived from *An Carraigín* – Little Rock. It is a parish situated in the barony of Clare, Co. Galway and was part of the Union of Headford and the diocese of Annaghdown.

The church is of no great interest or antiquity but its simple form may indicate a date ca. 10th century with some 12–13th century reconstruction. The present ruin is called *Seipul a Cargain* – The Chapel of Cargin, and was probably a chapel of ease to some of the saint's churches in the neighbouring parishes. There are also some remains of a circular enclosure around it (ca. 70m) and a children's burial ground. The church measures 10.4m L x 6m W.

above: Aumbry below: East window

South wall and pointed arch doorway

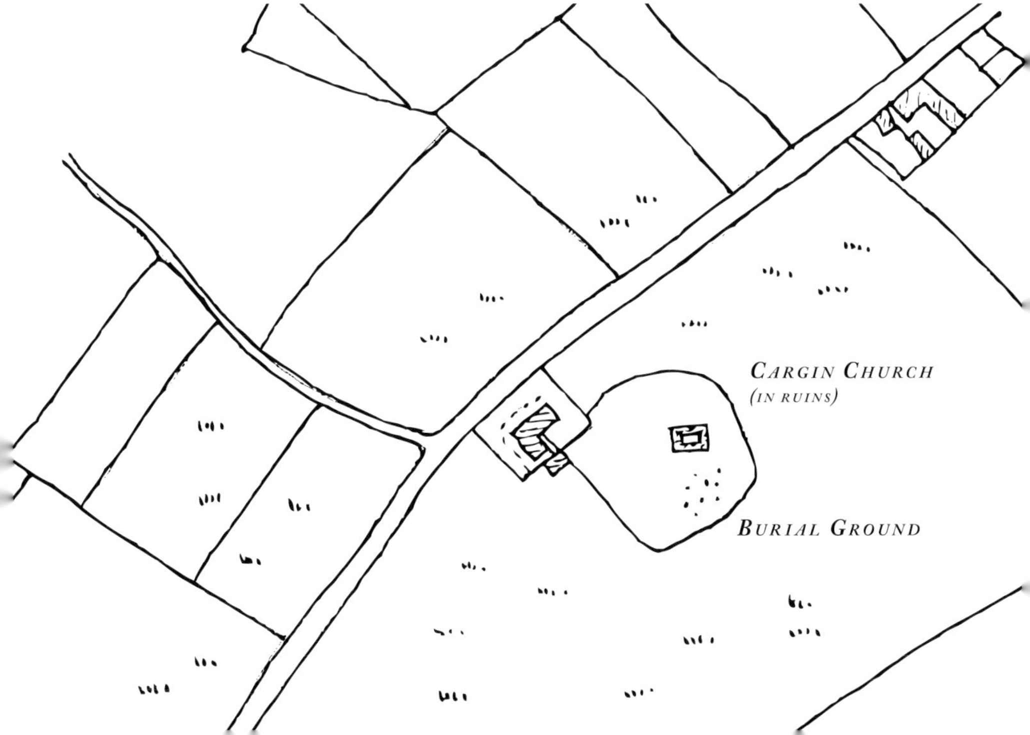

CARGIN CHURCH
(IN RUINS)

BURIAL GROUND

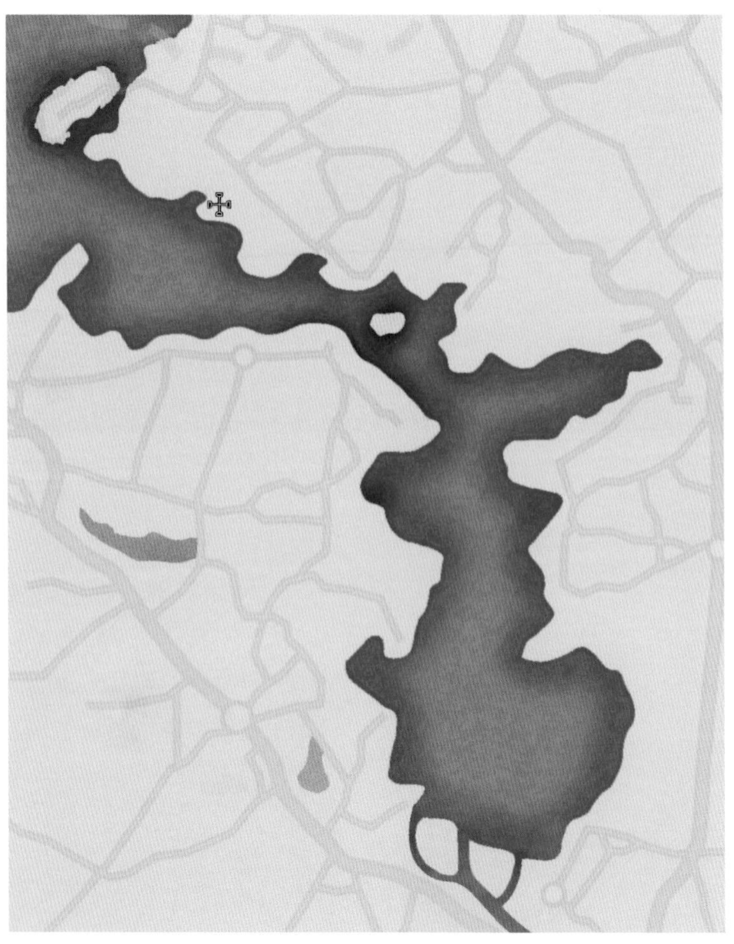

ANNAGHKEEN

N53 26’ W009 10’

According to Sir William Wilde writing in 1867; *‘A little to the east of the old castle (14th century) there are the vestiges of the church and burial ground of St Cronin’*. The only burial ground to be found here in Annaghkeen (*Eanach Caoin* – Pleasant Marsh) was a children’s burial ground situated a good way to the east, but there were no present indications or remains of a church amongst the stones. However, in a field slightly to the south east of the old Annaghkeen Castle, there is an oval shaped mound with evidence of bared stones at one end and on top of this mound, which may possibly be ancient remains of some description.

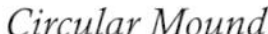

Circular Mound

The nearby burial ground (*see illustration above*) is however named as 'Kilcronan Burial Ground' (*Cill Cronáin* – Cronan's Church).

St Cronan Mochua (not to be confused with St Cronan of Roscrea) was the founder of the diocese of Balla which was subsequently merged into the diocese of Tuam. He lived during the period 596-637 but his history is also much recorded as a legendary character. He was however educated at Bangor, under St Comgall, and founded monasteries in Louth and Monaghan. He journeyed to Connacht in 616 and founded the church and abbey at Balla of which he was the first abbot-bishop. His Feast Day is celebrated on March 30th.

Remains of nearby Annaghkeen Castle and an unfinished O'Flaherty house

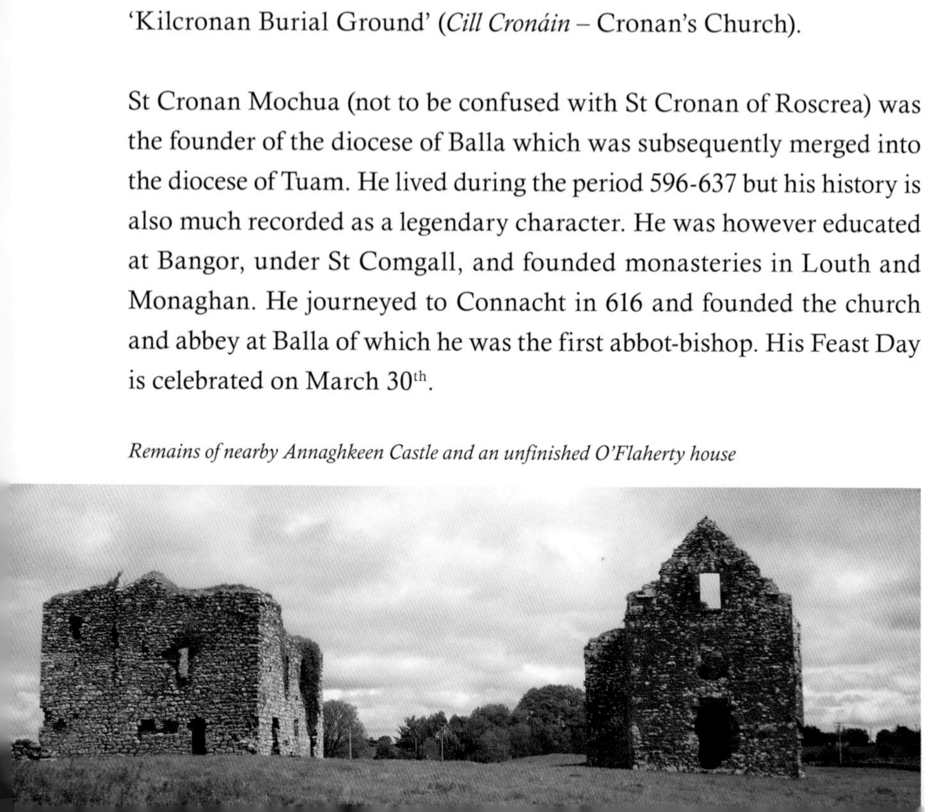

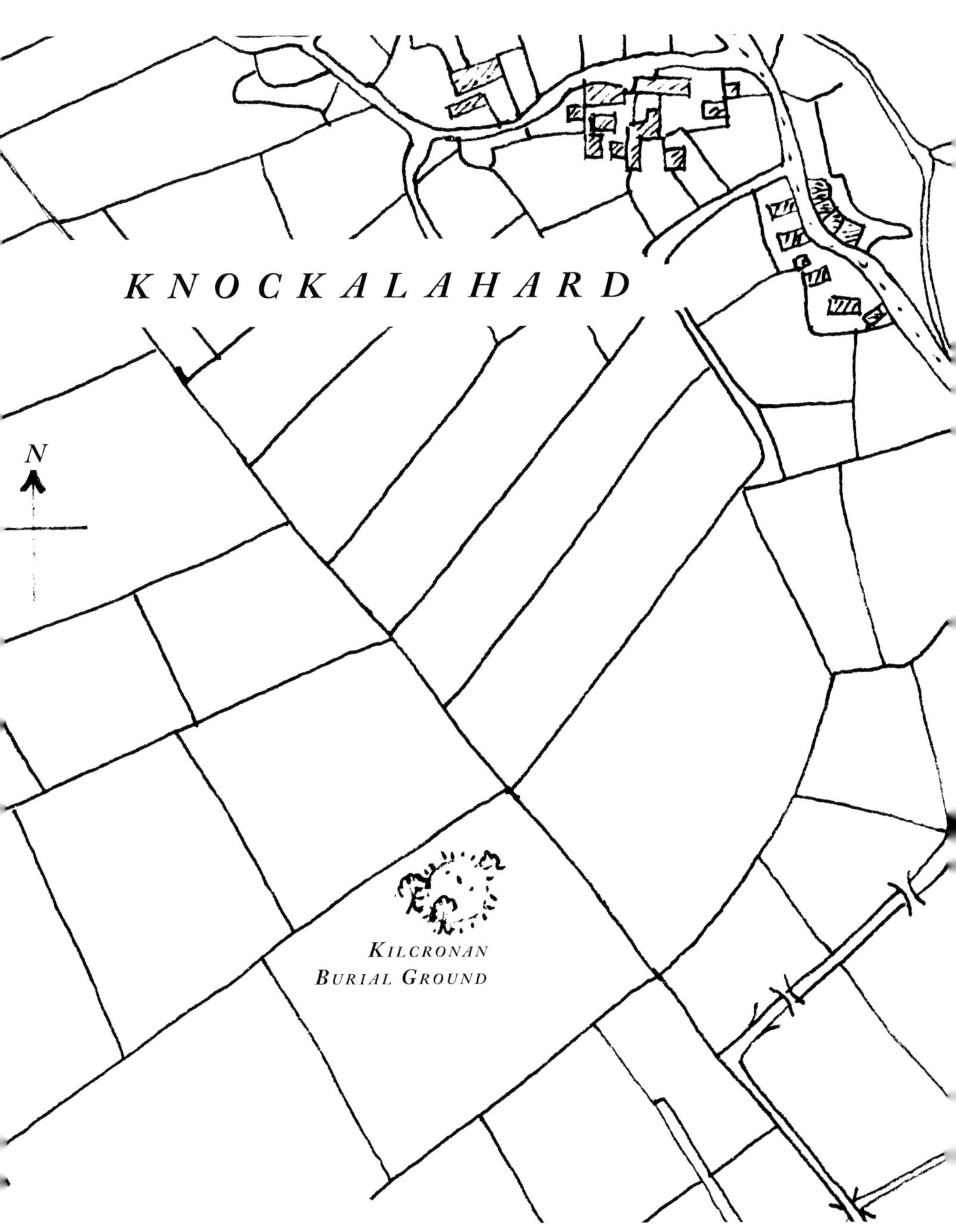
KNOCKALAHARD
N
KILCRONAN
BURIAL GROUND

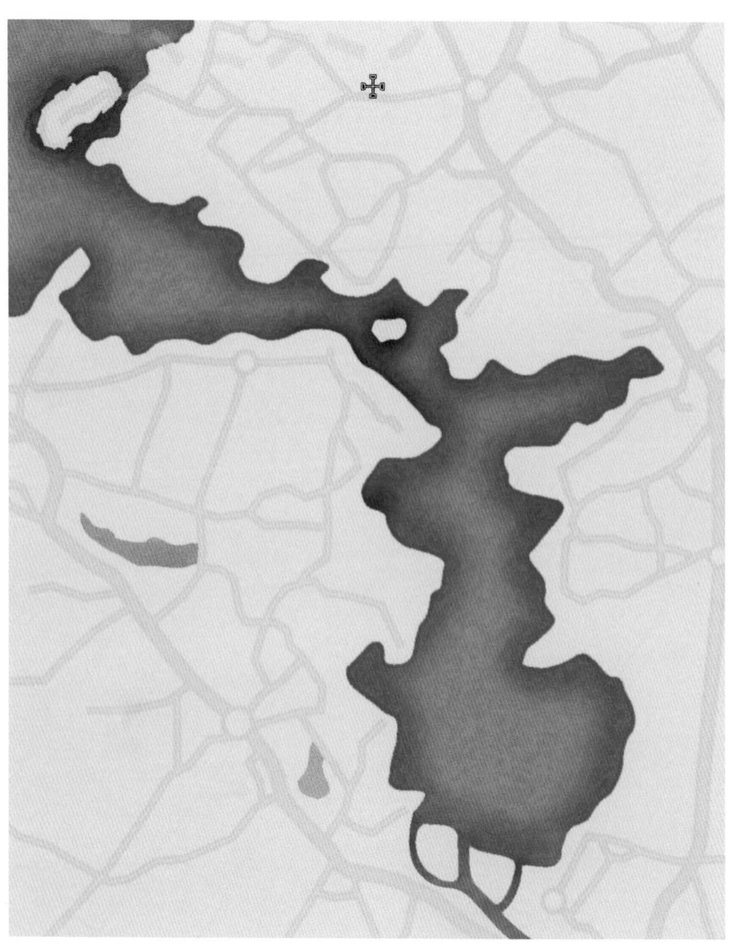

Killursa

N53°28 W009°08

Two miles west of Headford town on the north side of the Annaghkeen road are the ruins of *Cill Fhursa*, 'Church of Fursa', an ancient structure enlarged in medieval times and in the naming implies that the original was founded by St Fursey. Measuring 70' x 24' it has a Gothic pointed doorway and a large mullioned Gothic window, which indicates that the present structure was erected after the Norman invasion of 1169. The oldest and original part (ca. 620) is at the west end with a trabeate west doorway. This is a well kept structure surrounded by a modern and tidy burial ground.

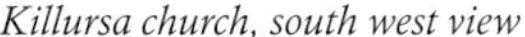

Killursa church, south west view

St Fursey, also known as Fursa, Fursy, Forseus or Furseus, and according to a 12th century written version of his life, was born at Rathmath on the island of Inchiquinn in Lough Corrib ca. 584 AD. However, another 12th century version places his birth possibly somewhere in Cavan. Nevertheless he was apparently the son of Fintan and grandson of Finlog, a pagan king. His mother was Gelges, the Christian daughter of Aed-Finn, King of Connacht, and was baptised by Brendan the Traveller who had founded the monastic settlement on Inchiquin island. He was later educated by the Inchiquin monks and ultimately entered the monastery in later years under the Abbot St Meldan, his soul friend *(anam cara).*

St Fursey was a man of great sanctity and is also known as someone who saw visions, the first of which made him famous in medieval literature as in the vision revealed to him of the state of man in sin and the beauty of virtue, and he received the injunction to become a more zealous labourer for the Lord. This ecstasy was renewed three nights later where he was taken to the heavens by three angels who contended six times with the demons for his soul. Among the spirits of those just made perfect he recognised saints Meldan and Beoan who gave him much spiritual instruction concerning the duties of ecclesiastics and monks and the dreadful effects of pride and disobedience. His brothers Foillan and Ultan joined the community at Rathmath, but Fursey seems to have renounced the administration of the monastery and to have devoted himself to preaching throughout the land, frequently exorcising evil spirits. Exactly twelve months later he received a third vision. This time the angel stayed with him a whole day, instructing him for his preaching, and prescribed for him twelve years of apostolic labour. This he faithfully fulfilled in Ireland, and then stripping himself of all earthly goods he retired for a time to a small

East window

Aumbry and south window

island in the ocean. After some years he then founded the monastery at Killursa near the shores of Lough Corrib.

After 630 AD Fursey left Ireland with his brothers Foillan and Ultan for Britain, where they were welcomed by the Christian king Sigeberht of East Anglia. They assisted Sigeberht and Felix in Christianising the kingdom and in introducing monasticism. About 640 Fursey founded the monastery of Cnoberesburgh, near modern Yarmouth in Norfolk, which became the centre of his ministry. He sailed to Gaul some time between 640 and 644 and established himself in Neustria (present day Normandy), where he was well received by Clovis II. In about 644 he founded a monastery at Lagny, near Paris. On a later journey (652) he died at the village of Mezerolles. He was struck down there by illness, a place where he had restored the Duke Haymon's son to life, after which the village was named Forsheim (Pforzheim), which translates as the House of Fursey. Later his body was transferred to Péronne, where his shrine became a great pilgrimage site and the monastery there remained an Irish centre through the 8th century.

above: Internal view of west gable

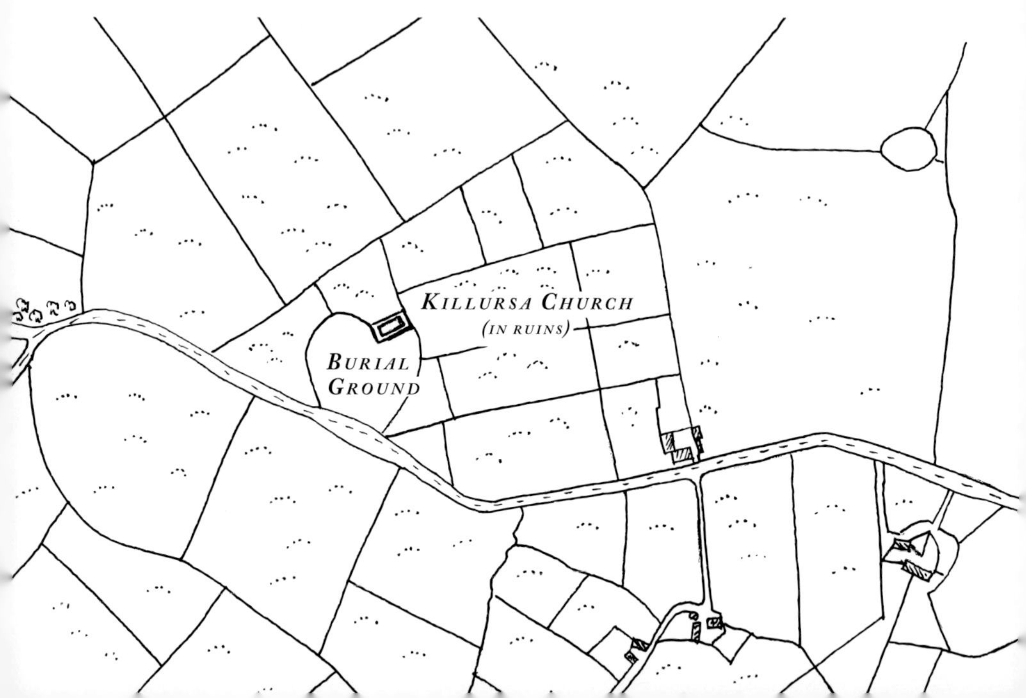

Killursa Church
(in ruins)

Burial
Ground

Fursey's visions, which he was said to have experienced throughout his life, became widely known through accounts by the Venerable Bede in his *Ecclesiastical History of the English People* (8th century), which also contains the earliest life of Fursey written by an anonymous contemporary monk, and by Aelfric Garammaticus (10th century). The visions included demoniac assaults, conversations with angels, divinations and glimpses of heaven and hell. He was the patron saint of the O'Flahertys and his Feast Day is January 16th.

above left: External trabeate door above right: Internal view
below left: External view on south wall below right: Internal south wall window

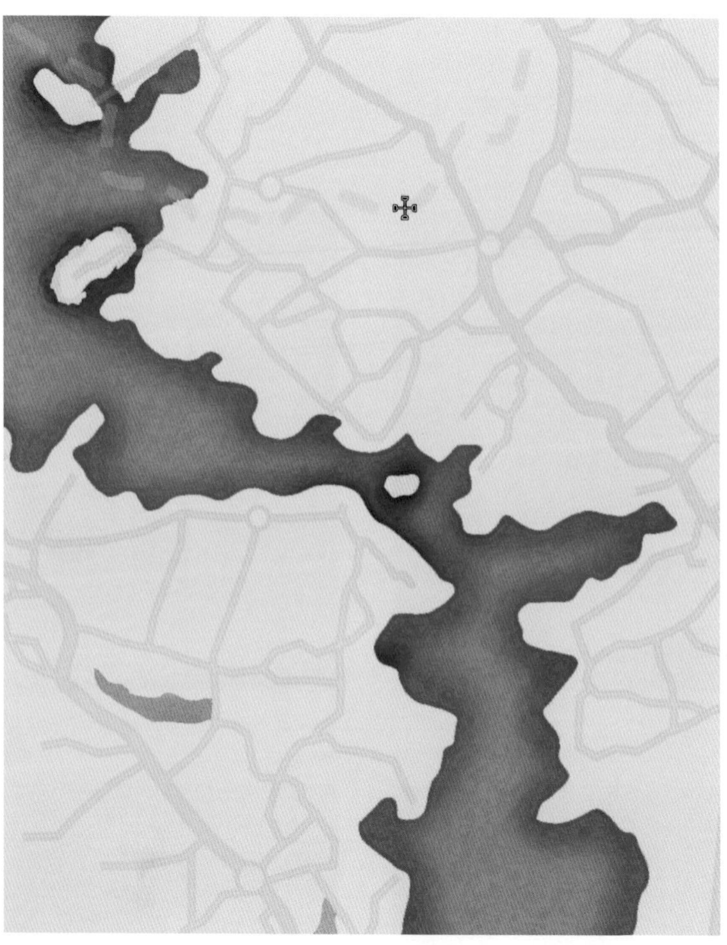

ROSS ERRILLY

N53 28' W009 07'

This magnificent ecclesiastical structure is not strictly an early Christian site as it only had its origins in 1270 but was not properly founded until 1351, then adopting the Reformed Franciscan Rule in 1470 and becoming Observantine. It was then greatly enlarged 28 years later. Although they suffered repression in 1538 they were helped by many friends, including the great Church of Ireland Archbishop of Tuam, Dr. O'Donnell, to return here seven times between that date and 1753, after which they finally departed to an adjacent island in the Black River, where the ruins of their temporary dwellings are still to be seen.

Ross Errilly Friary with Lough Corrib in background - photo courtesy of Liam Donoghue

However, this Friary includes a special mention in this book as it is truly one of the most magnificent and best preserved late monastic ruins in Ireland and which, practically complete in every detail, could easily be re-occupied with just a new roof! The one drawback to such an event is commented upon by Richard Hayward in his book *The Corrib Country*: *'If it weren't for those ghastly, vulgar and almost indecent modern tombs, which are here uglier and more unsightly than in almost any other place'*. He comments in a similar manner concerning the ancient Abbey of Knockmoy, located west of Tuam:

> *'[…] if you will but look for the cloisters at Knockmoy you will see that they have been virtually obliterated by that foul bane of all Irish monastic remains, the prescriptive right of certain families to burial in these sacred places. There is barely an ecclesiastical ruin in Ireland that is not choked from end to end, and from side to side, with ugly, and often outrageously vulgar, modern tombstones, and I am afraid the sentiment against casting them out of a place from which any sense of public decency would always have excluded them, is too strong to be gainsaid.'*

I have also found this to be tragically true in one, albeit beautifully kept ancient ruin in Connemara, where the perpetrators actually cut away the ancient altar stone in half to accommodate an ugly modern headstone!

The official name for this Friary is *Mainistir an Rois*, Monastery of the Wooded Headland. However, the Four Masters named it as *Mainistir Ros Oirbhealach* (or *Oirialaigh*), adding the interpretation that it lies on the eastern way or route.

below: Interior next pages: Aerial view of interior - photo courtesy of Liam Donoghue

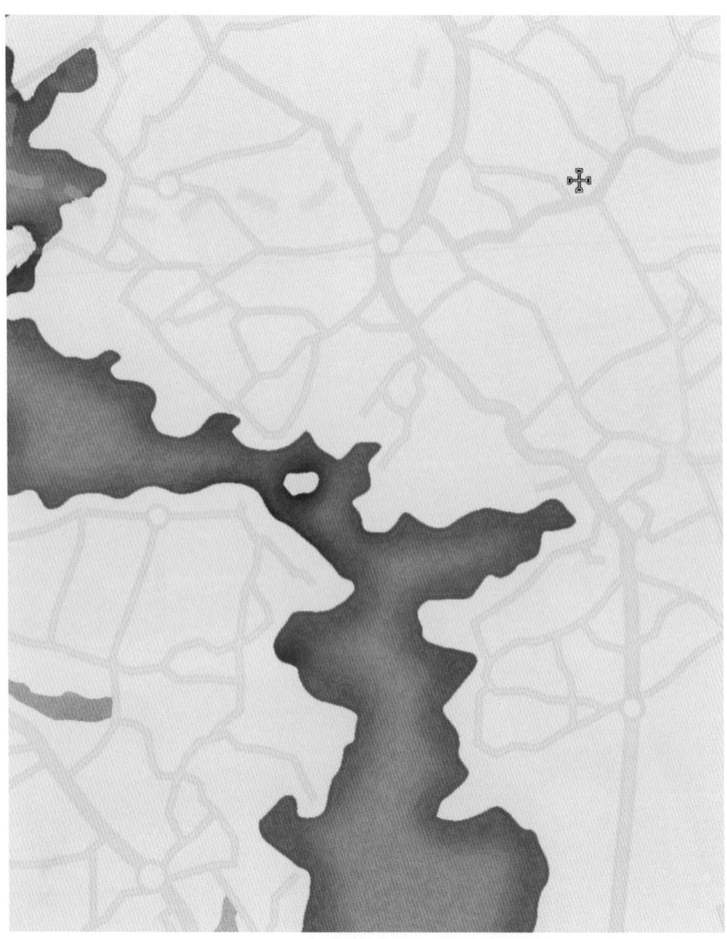

Donaghpatrick

N53°28' W009°02'

About 4km east of Headford town and on the left of the main road towards Caherlistrane can be found the recently preserved ruins of a fine, partly built 12th century church, which stands on the site of the original 5th century Patrician church.

West gable and south wall - photo courtesy of Liam Donoghue

It is held that St Patrick established this church as a headquarters for his mission in this area and which became the Ecclesia Dominica Patricii – the principal church of St Patrick – hence the Donagh (*Domhnach Pádraig*) Patrick – the chief, geographical, historical and central church in that whole area of *Maigh Seola*. Tradition says that St Patrick journeyed

Aerial view (detail) - photo courtesy of Liam Donoghue

from *Cruacha* through Dunmore and Kilbannon to Donaghpatrick, then northward crossing the Black River into the territory of *Cuil Toladh*. The natural ford over which he passed would have been at Shrule, the traditional crossing from *Maigh Seola* on the south. Prior to his crossing he had visited the chieftain of *Maigh Seola* near Lough Cime, now Lough Hacket, and also founded this church where he left his disciple, bishop Felartus, in charge.

below left: Interior view below right: West gable and south wall opposite page: North door

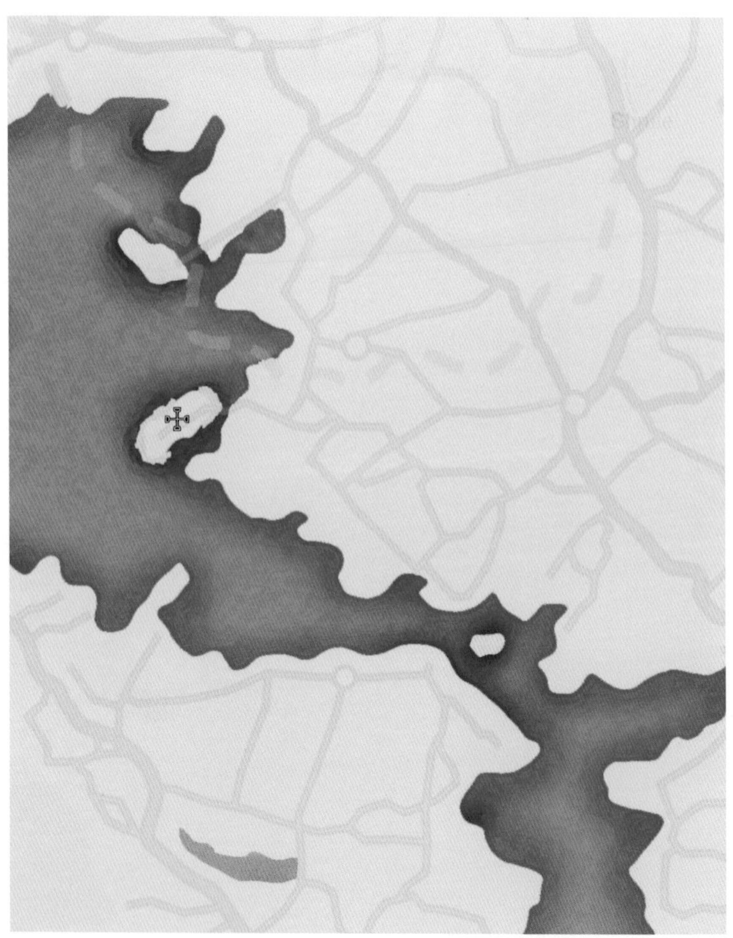

INCHIQUINN

N53°27 W009°13

The island of Inchiquinn (*Inis Mhic Uí Chuinn* – Island of the Descendant of Conn), in the parish of Killursa, is the site of an Early Christian monastery reputedly founded by St Brendan the Navigator. It is possible he had accompanied St Patrick at Inchagoill Island (*see Luguaedon Stone, page 19*). The Island also contains an ancient burial ground known as 'Rathmath' (*Rath Maith* – The Kindly Enclosure).

Aerial view of Inchiquinn Island - photo courtesy of Liam Donoghue

Faint foundation lines of a building, possibly a church, can be seen at the north east end of the island close to the shore. It is rectangular in plan (E-W 7.6m L x 4.7m W) but no architectural features survive. This spot is still respected locally but no visible trace of the burial ground survives.

above: Aerial view of the field where the original oratory was supposed to be below: Ground view

In spite of the paucity of any ecclesiastical remains, this island appears to have a monastic legacy and importance far beyond its size and in the number of saints associated with the island.

Firstly, as previously stated, the original settlement is said to have been founded by St Brendan the Navigator, who was born in 484 AD in Ciarraight Luachra, near Tralee in Co. Kerry, and baptised at Tubrid, near Ardfert, by Bishop Erc. From the age of one he was nurtured and instructed for five years in the care of St Ita at Killeedy (*Cill Íde* – Ita's Church). At six he was sent to St Jarlath's monastery school at Tuam where he received a theological education that led, at the age of 28, to his ordination in 512 under the hand of Bishop Erc.

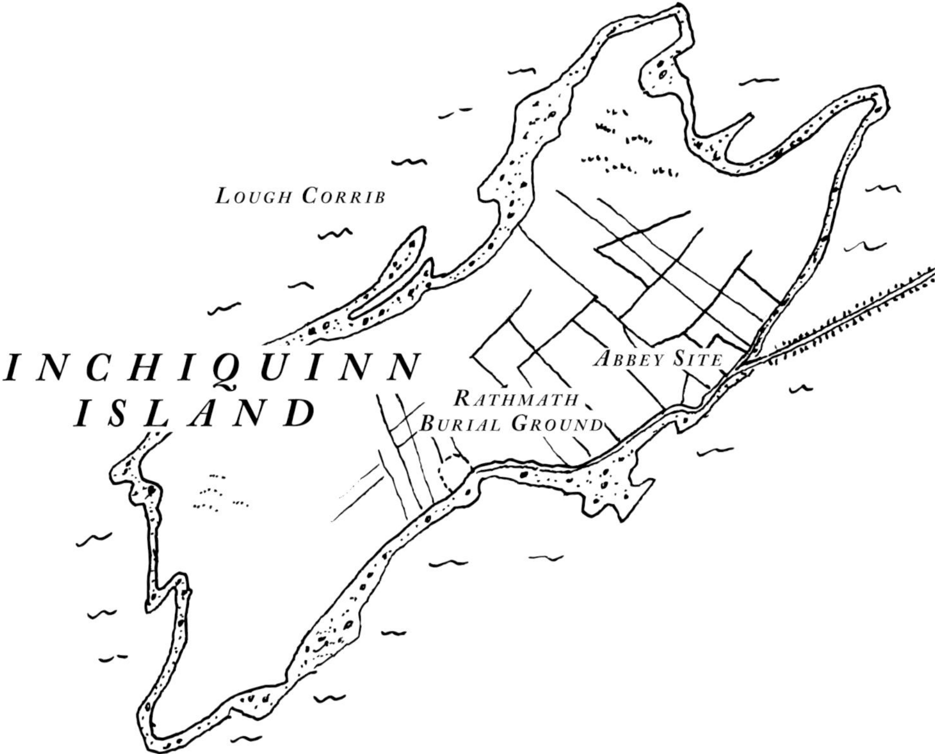

St Brendan and his brethren setting sail, Artist unknown. From Rev. Denis O'Donoghue, St Brendan the Voyager (Dublin: Brown & Nolan, 1893) frontispiece

His overriding reputation was as a traveller and rested on the *Navigatio Sancti Brendani Abbatis* – The Voyage of St Brendan the Abbot, an account compiled by an Irish monk in the 9th century from the various oral traditions that were in circulation. According to one account, St Brendan was granted a vision of the 'Promised Land' from the top of Mt. Brandon, after which he constructed his leather clad boat and with some 14 crew of fellow monks set sail in 530 on a voyage lasting 7 years, taking them to Iceland, Greenland and to the American mainland. Although he was in his fifties on his return he continued in his missionary zeal to found monastic communities on Coney Island on the river Shannon, Inchiquin Island on Lough Corrib, Annaghdown, Co. Galway and at Clonfert. He also had Foundations in Scotland, Wales, Brittany, the Faroe Islands, Germany and elsewhere. His most celebrated foundation is at Clonfert where he is buried and which is referred to in the chapter Annaghdown (*see page 83*).

Another of the most famous of Irish monks was St Fursey who was born at Rathmath on Inchiquin Island ca. 570 AD, baptised by St Brendan and later educated at the monastery on Inchiquin under its abbot, St Meldan. A fuller account of St Fursey or Fursa is given in the chapter on his foundation at Killursa (*see page 109*). It is also held by some that his brothers were St Ultan, St Enda (*see chapter on Killagoola page 67*), St Cunna (*see chapter on Kilcoona page 95*), and St Foillan, although any doubts concerning this relativity may arise from the fact that Foillan is also described as the 'uterine brother' of Fursey, meaning that they had the same mother, but not the same father. The connection with Inchiquin may certainly be as a family base if not the actual birthplace of each of these brothers, together with the fact that they all seem to have spent time under tutelage in St Brendan's monastery, probably under St Meldan who was Brendan's successor.

St Ultan, as with St Foillan, was the son of the royal woman Gelges, herself a daughter of King Aed of Connacht (possibly *Áed mac Echach*). In the *Ecclesiastical History of the English People* (The Venerable Bede) it relates that Ultan joined the mission led by Fursa which went from Ireland through British territory to East Anglia in around 633 AD, to the kingdom of King Sigeberht of East Anglia. The monastery of which he was a member there was established in the precinct of an old Roman stone-built shore-fort near the sea, at a place called Cnobheres-burg. The king received them and endowed the monastery, and it was later re-endowed by King Anna of East Anglia and his nobles. The site is commonly identified with Burgh Castle (Norfolk) near the mouth of the river Yare, thought to be Garianonum of the *Notitia Dignitatum* and with the geographical description of Britain by Claudius Ptolemy.

After several years in which he served a probation in the monastery at Cnobheresburg, Ultan went off to live alone in East Anglia as a hermit. In around 643 Fursey handed his duties to Foillan and went to join Ultan, taking nothing with him, and they lived for a year together by the labour of their hands in a life of contemplation and philosophy. However the kingdom was disturbed by inroads of heathens, and Fursey left East Anglia in around 644, entrusting the monastery in East Anglia and its brethren to his brother Foillan. After being welcomed by Erchinoald at Péronne and by Clovis II and Queen Balthild, Fursey was granted an estate at Lagny on the Marne, where he built his monastery.

A record preserved at Nivelles shows that Foillan and his brethren, including Ultan, fled the kingdom of East Anglia with the help of King Anna in 651, when the monastery was under attack from King Penda of Mercia, and King Anna himself was exiled from his own kingdom. Foillan and Ultan took away the precious property and books of the monastery, and after unhappy dealings with Erchinoald, they were received by Ste Gertrude of Nivelles and her mother Itta. Foillan went off to found a monastery at Fosses in Namur with the encouragement and support of Itta, but was murdered with some companions not long afterwards by bandits, during a journey from Nivelles to Fosses. St Ultan died in 657 and his Feast Day is kept on May 1st.

St Foillan, like many other Irish monks who went to the Continent in the 7th century, was invested with Episcopal dignity, having possibly been a monastic bishop in Cnosberesgurg. He was therefore of great assistance in the organisation of worship, and the holy books and relics which he brought were great treasures for St Itta and St Gertrude. As the monastery of Nivelles was under Irish discipline, the companions of Foillan were well received and lived side by side with the holy women, occupying themselves with the details of worship under the general direction of the abbess.

Through the liberality of Itta, Foillan was enabled to build a monastery at Fosses-la-Ville, not far from Nivelles, in the province of Namur. After the death of Itta in 652, Foillan came one day to Nivelles and sang Mass, on the eve of the feast of St Quentin. The ceremony being finished,

above: Collégiale Saint-Feuillien, Fosses-la-Ville, Namur - photo by Jean-Pol Grandmont
below: Relics of St-Feuillien kept in Fosses-la-Ville - photo courtesy of Guy Reynaerts

next page: Coat of arms of St-Pholien-des-Prés in Liege - illustration by Jean-Denys Boussart showing St-Pholien and other symbols of the city of Liege - note that the designer made a point of giving him the Irish style tonsure which involved shaving the front of the hairline, not the round tonsure usual on the Continent (special thanks to historian Catherine Jennings)

Commune Libre de Saint-Pholien-des-Prés
Sint-Fogin, Li Porotche dès braves djins

he resumed his journey, doubtless undertaken in the interests of his monastery. However, in the Sonian Forest the saint and his companions fell into a trap set by bandits who inhabited the dense forest. They were slain, stripped, and their bodies concealed. According to local tradition Foillan's head, still speaking prayers, was thrown into a nearby pigsty (ca. 650). The bodies were later recovered by St Gertrude, and when she had taken some relics of the saint, his body was borne to the monastery of Fosses-la-Ville, where it was buried ca. 655.

Foillan was one of the numerous Irish travellers who, in the course of the 7th century, evangelised in Neustria, bringing there the liturgy and sacred vessels, founding prosperous monasteries, and sharing considerably in the propagation of the faith in these countries. Owing to the friendship which united him with Erchinoald, Mayor of the Palace, and with the members of the royal family of Pepin, Foillan played a significant part in Frankish ecclesiastical history, as shown by his share in the direction of Nivelles and by the foundation of the monastery of Fosses-la-Ville.

It is therefore not surprising that he should be honoured and venerated both at Nivelles and Fosses-la-Ville and to find at Le Roeulx in Belgium, a monastery bearing his name. As late as the 12th century, the veneration in which he was held inspired the Abbott of Esperance to compose a lengthy biography of the saint. He is also the patron of Fosses near Charleroi, in the diocese of Namur. His feast is celebrated on October 31st and in the diocese of Mechlin and the diocese of Tournai, on November 5th. His name is often represented as Faelan, Faolan, Foelan, Pholien and Feuillien (in French). According to historian Catherine Jennings of Carna, who has also attended the celebrations in memory of St Foillan in Belgium, the church in Liege is dedicated to St-Pholien as well as having a town there named after him.

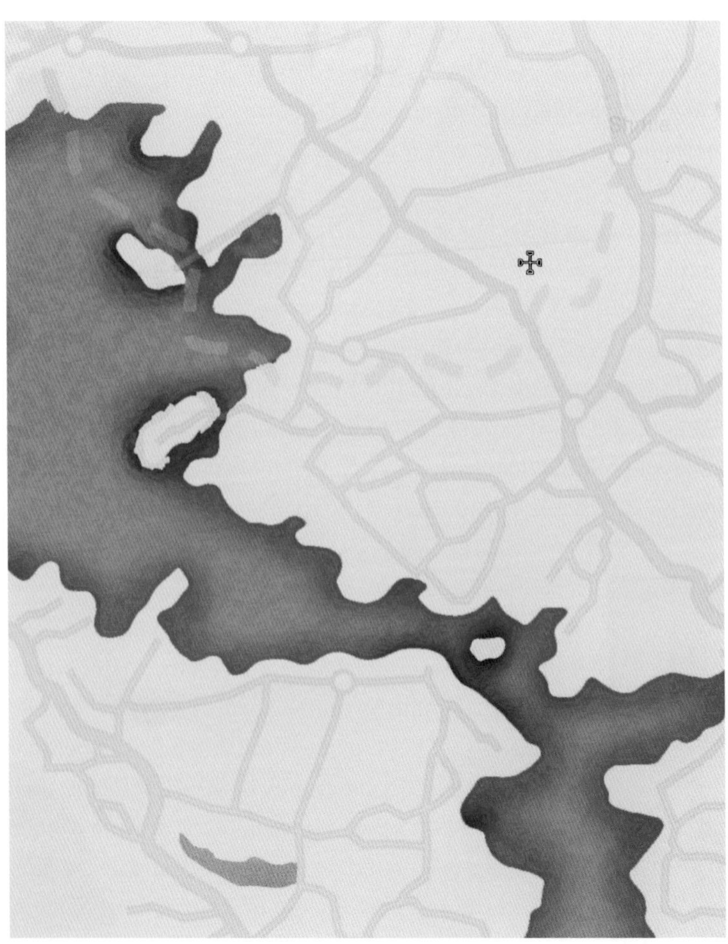

Kinlough

N53°29 W009°06

Just over a mile directly north of Headford town can be found the ruins of both Kinlough Church and Castle (*Ciona Locha* – Head of the Lake). On one side of the Owen Dubh river on a rise is the ruined 13th century church incorporating a square belfry at the western end. The remains of three lancet windows can be seen in the east gable. The structure is presently scaffolded in order to carry out some preservation to this large ruin.

Church and castle - photo courtesy of Liam Donoghue

The church measures 65' L x 22'4" W and belongs to the Gothic style which superseded the Romanesque, and this was in the 13th century. Apparently and together with similar churches in Shrule and Moyne, Kinlough stood in 1306.

left page: South aerial view of church above: Kinlough Castle - photos courtesy of Liam Donoghue

On the other side of the river stand the ruins of an imposing castle built in the 16th century by the Burkes. In 1574, it was in the possession of McWilliam Eighter (Sir John fitz Oliver Burke). According to the Annalists, some parts of the original castle may have been erected as early as 1228. Notable are the tall profiled chimney-stacks servicing two corner fireplaces.

These two ancient buildings are in State ownership.

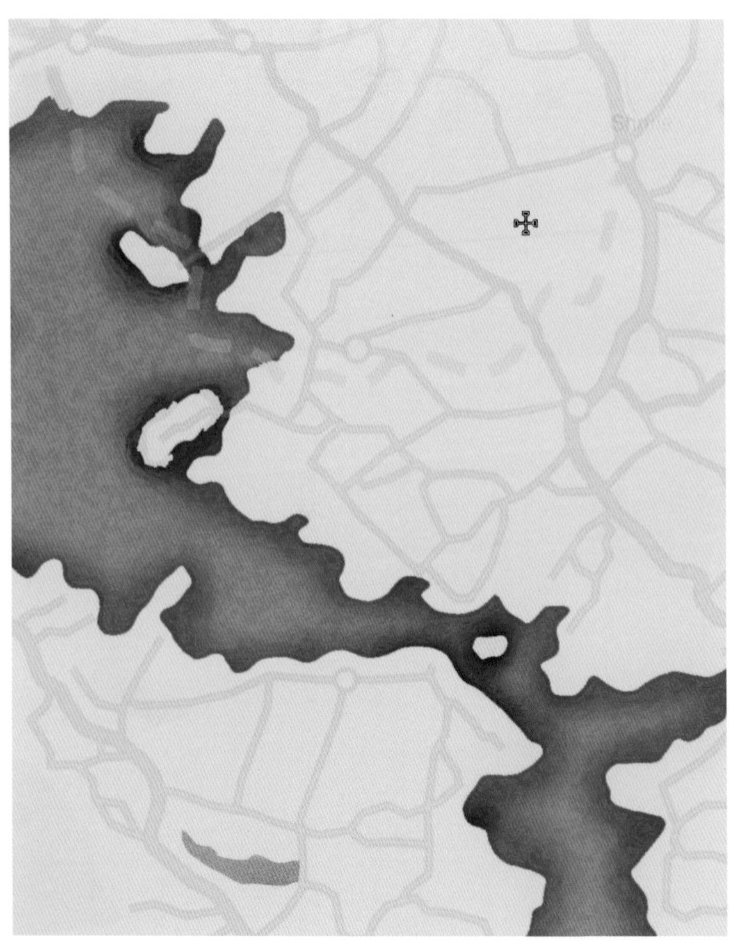

N53 29' W009 07'

Six kilometres east of Lough Corrib in the civil parish of Shrule stands the well-kept graveyard and ruined church of Moyne (*Maigin or Maighin,* 'a little farmstead'). This is a remarkable early site which has one of the largest ecclesiastical enclosures of its type in the country measuring 380' L x 330' W with the cashel (wall) 8' W and 7' H. The present church ruins belong to the early Gothic ca. 12th century, but is believed to be originally Irish Romanesque from the 10th century or earlier. The church measures 52' L x 21' W and is situated on a little height near the centre of the oval enclosure which itself is in good condition.

Aerial view of ecclesiastical enclosure

above: View of graveyard and church - photo courtesy of Liam Donoghue

Relatively recent excavations revealed pits, ditches and a lintel grave of early Christian date. As well as the early church and graveyard these enclosures would contain the dwellings and workshops of a community sometimes approaching the size of a small town. Such buildings would generally have been of wood, hence there are no remains, and there would have been further divisions within the enclosure.

below left: South door below right: East window

above: Standing stones at north west below: Section of enclosure wall

below: South west aerial view

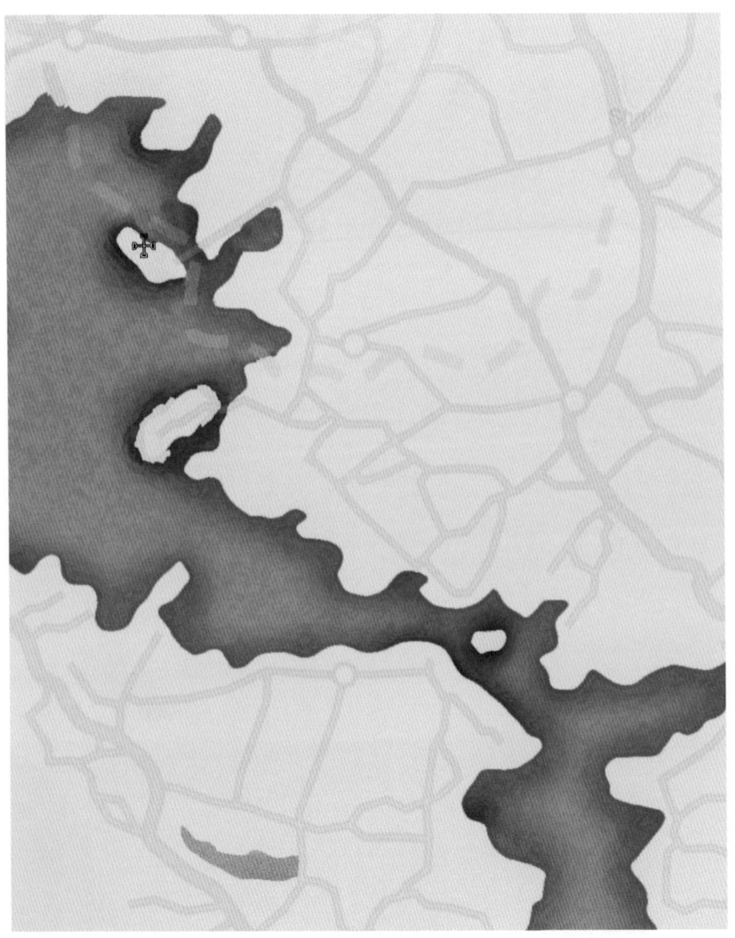

INISHMICATREER

N53°29 W009°15

On the north east side of the island of Inishmicatreer (*Inis Mhic an Triúr* – Island of the Son of the Three or, The Trinity), which is accessible via a causeway, are the early ecclesiastical remains of a ruined Abbey which is depicted on the OS map (1922) as a large oval enclosure (N-S 130m x E-W 135m) defined by a lane and field walls.

Aerial view of children's burial ground at center right and probable walls of original enclosure

No visible surface trace survives of it, or the 'Abbey' and 'Tower' shown in the interior. Neither is there any trace of the 'Grave Yard', also named on the OS map, though there is a tradition of a Children's Burial Ground at the site which is depicted above and overleaf.

above: Entrance to burial ground below: Remaining wall of ecclesiastical structure

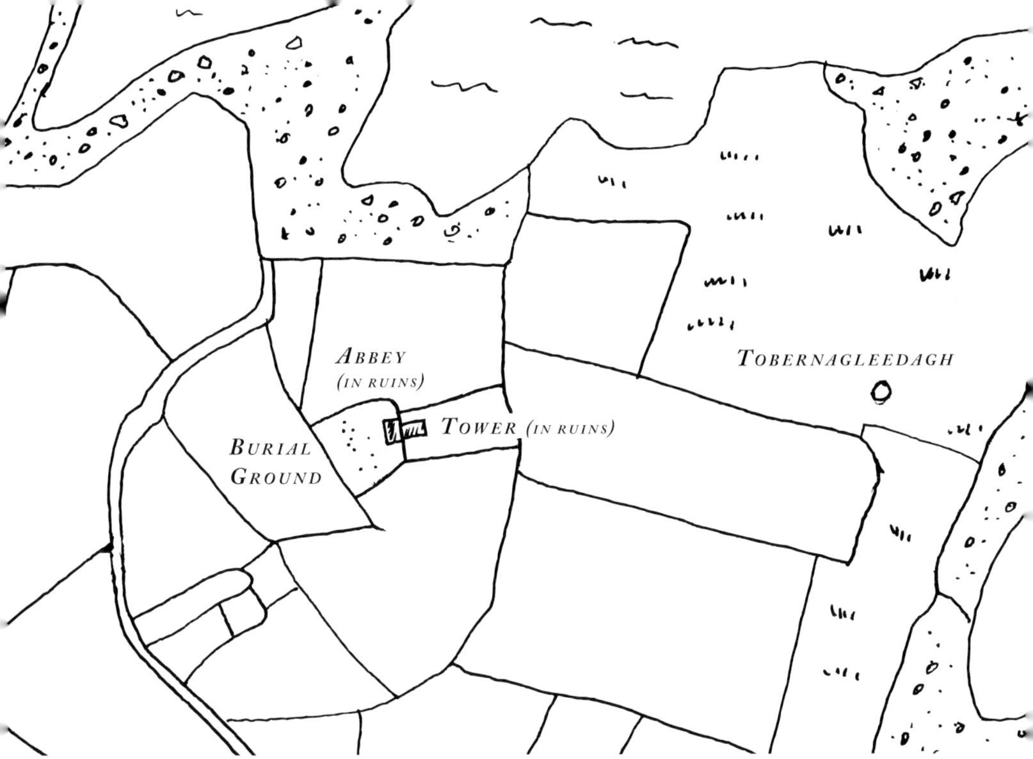

ABBEY
(IN RUINS)
TOBERNAGLEEDAGH
TOWER (IN RUINS)
BURIAL
GROUND

above: Map showing the circular boundary of probable original enclosure below: Burial stones

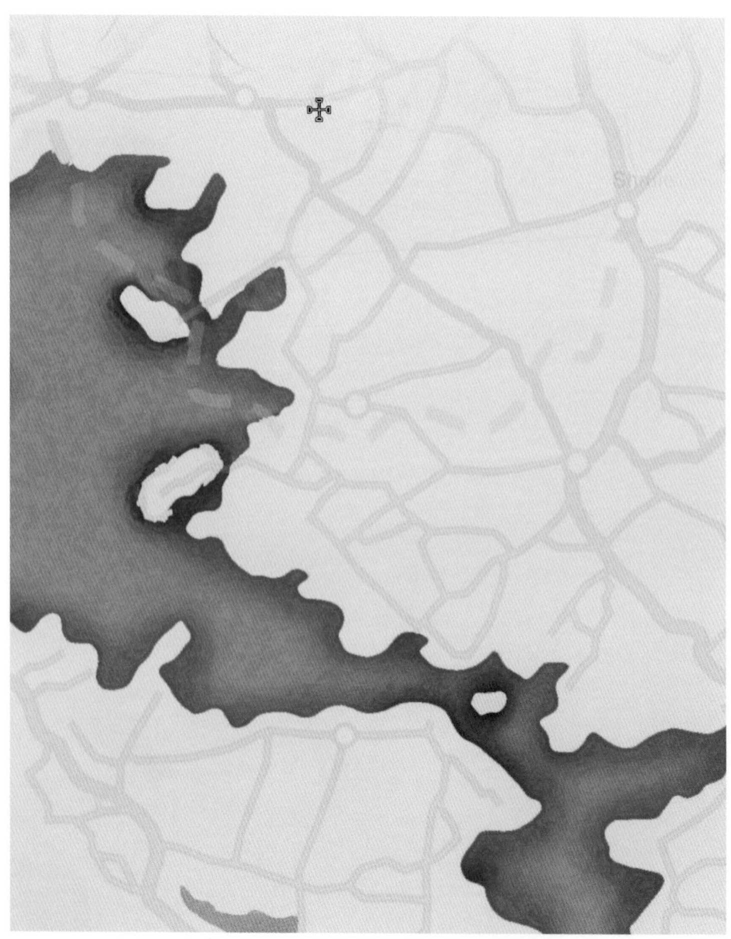

CROSS

N53°32 W009°11

Approximately half a mile to the north-east of the village of Cross (*An Chrois* – The Cross), adjacent to and on the road to Kilmaine, stand the ruins of a once joined and most interesting castle and church. Known locally as the Castle of Cross, there are the ruins of an early Gothic church once attached to its eastern side. The castle, or tower, which was very well and solidly built, has a narrow light on each face but the once pointed doorway leading from the church has now sadly collapsed. It is

West view of tower and church

presumed this tower would have been built at the same time as the church to serve as a residence for the clergy, a belfry, a security for valuables and as a defensive structure. Many other early churches in Ireland would also have had similar defensive structures such as the round towers were believed to be. Today, this little complex is surrounded by only a relatively modest enclosure.

The church itself measures 40' long and 19' wide on the inside. The remaining northern wall is 13'6" high and the east gable is still standing with its magnificent double-lighted eastern window. In this gable we can see that apart from the chiselled stone between the lights and their outer edges, the inner window jambs, splays and soffits are cleverly constructed of well selected uncut blocks and the remaining wall is finely constructed with undressed and small stones. At the base of the wall is also a solid arch of undressed stone carrying the weight of the above structure.

View of east gable

This structure is situated in the townland of Attyickard, otherwise properly known as *Áit Tí Riocáird*, 'The Site of Richard's House', indicating that possibly a Burke had been involved in the construction of the tower.

above left: West view showing recently collapsed doorway of tower right: Aumbry in north wall

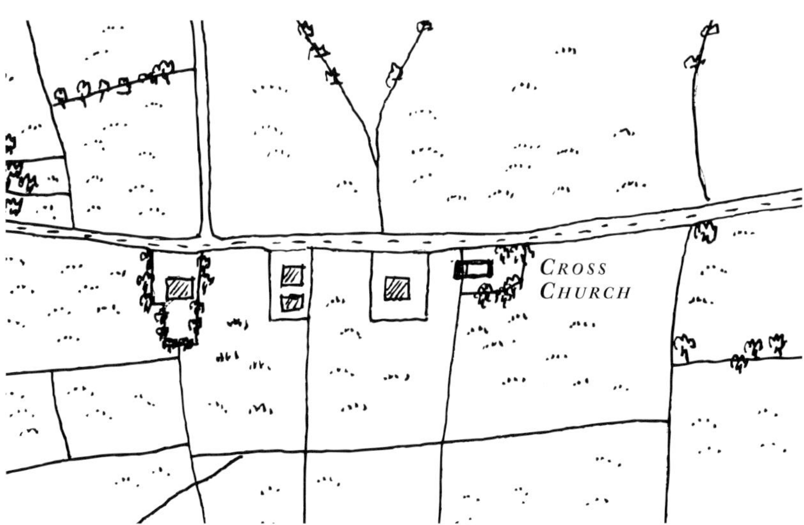

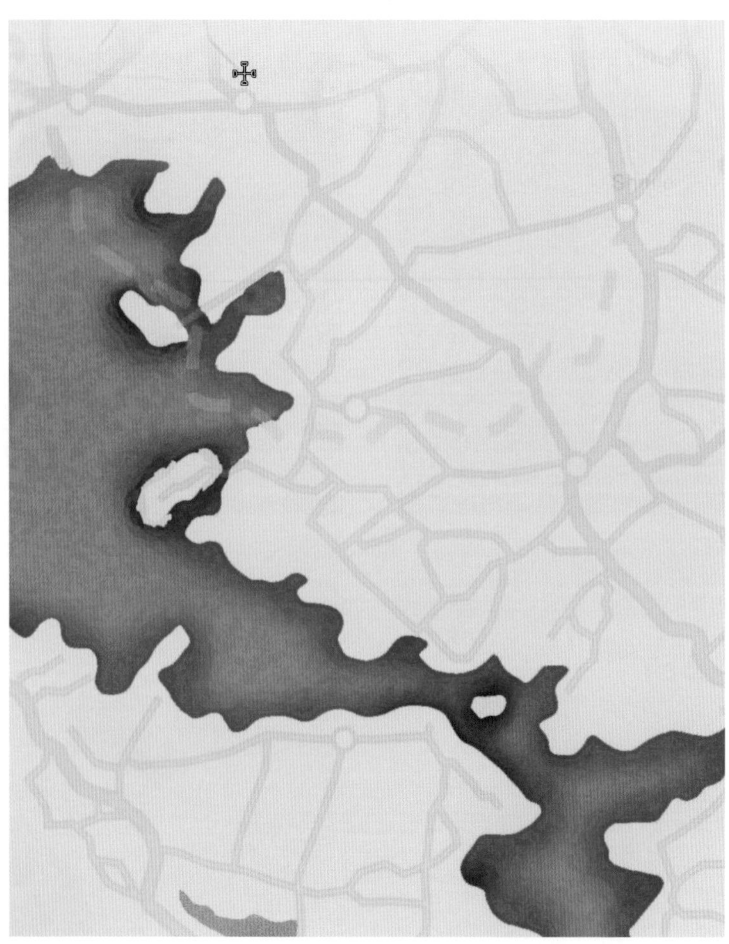

N53°32 W009°13

Behind Dowagh House in the townland of Dowagh East (*Dumhach* – A Misty Place), standing in the middle of an ancient circular burial ground which itself is surrounded by pasture, is the much ruined oratory dedicated to *St Fraochán* (Frughaun), whose Feast Day is celebrated on November 20th.

Enclosure wall and oratory at centre

Fraochán became bishop of Boclune *(Bo-cluain*) near Leix. But the most important monastery of ancient Leix was however founded by St Fintan (603) originally of Headford, Co. Galway and located on the *Slige Dala*, one of the great roads of ancient times, which ensured its importance in Early Medieval Ireland. Today there are two graveyards there, the ruins of an early church and a recently fallen 'penny tree'. The tree was said to have a cavity in its trunk where water was found. This so-called well of St Fintan was believed to have had healing properties ascribed to it. Interesting also that the meaning of *Fraochán* in English is 'bilberry', whilst *Bo-cluain* means a fertile spot or a cow meadow.

West gable and remains of trabeate door

West gable and south wall

South wall and collapsed east gable

The Dowagh oratory is one of the oldest of the Cyclopean churches in Ireland. Its square headed doorway is sadly collapsed and only one side still stands together with most of the south wall. The remains indicate an internal measurement of (EW) 5.50m x (NS) 3.70m. Apparently it was also divided into an upper and lower apartment by a flat floor and two of the corbels still remain. This was rare in this style of oratory and may have been where the monk lived. Below the collapsed east end is a spring well which feeds into the Cross river.

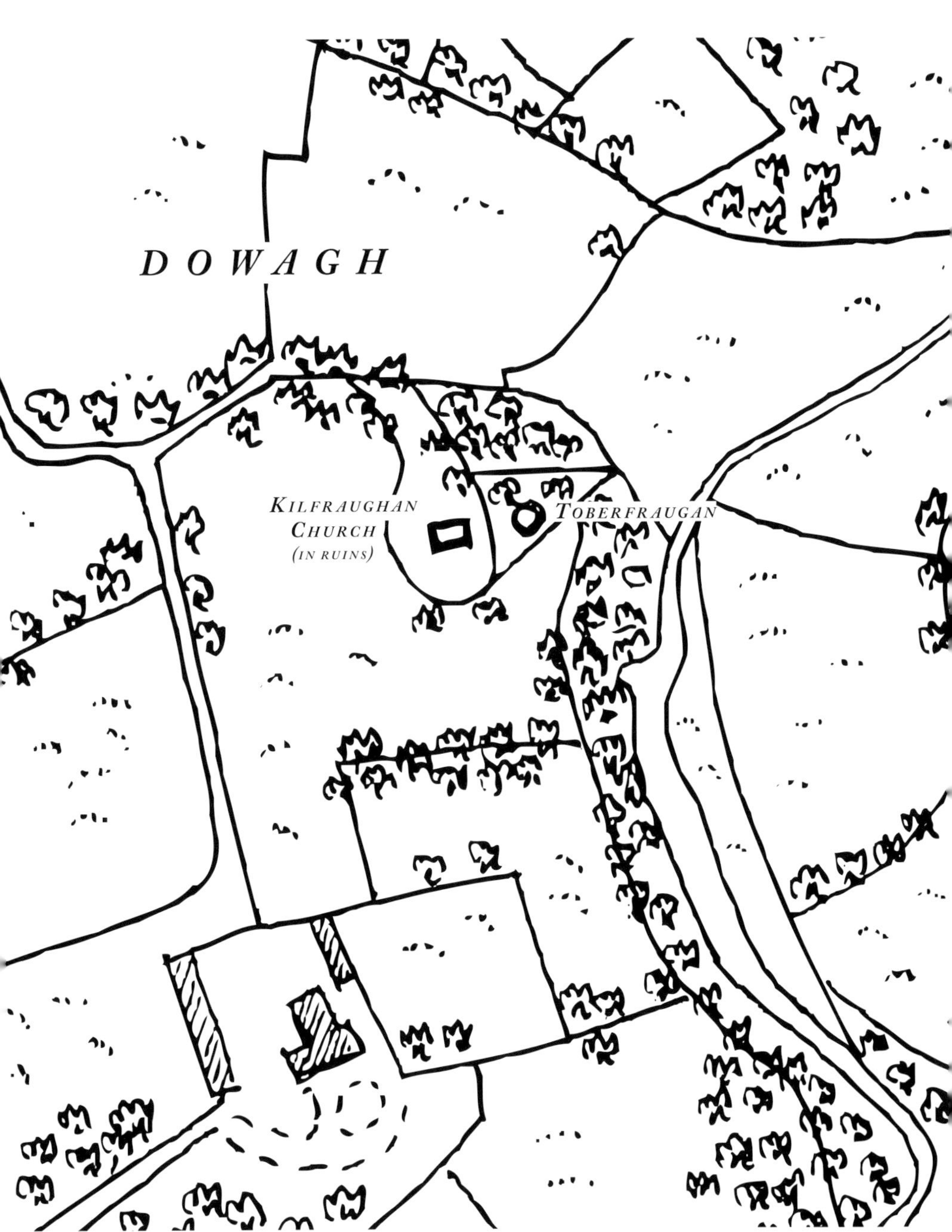
DOWAGH
KILFRAUGHAN
CHURCH
(IN RUINS)
TOBERFRAUGAN

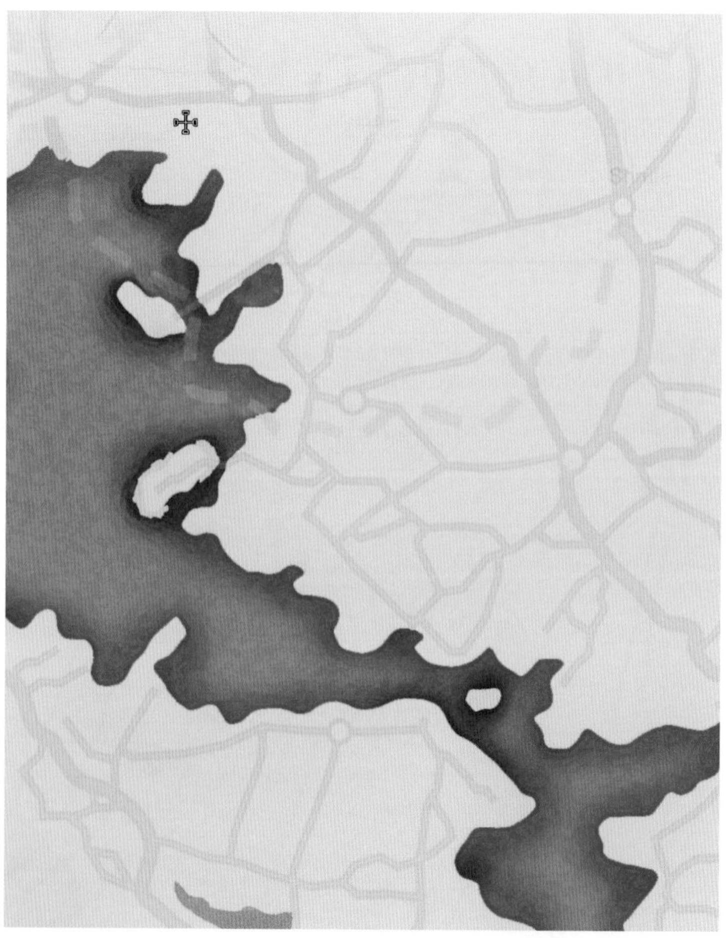

Killarsagh

N53 32' W009 44'

To the left of the main Cross to Cong road and on the right hand side of the by-road leading down to the lake in the townland of Ballymacgibbon North, in Cross, Co. Mayo, stand the ruins of *Cill Ársa* – Ancient Church. It stands heavily overgrown with trees, bushes and briars as well as being practically flooded on the south side by a badly drained stream. According to Sir William Wilde it would measure internally 24' long by 16.5' wide. Some of the east gable still appears to remain although heavily hidden and it has a round-headed window very similar to that in St Brecan's church in Rosscahill on the opposite side of the lake. The name is so similar to that of Killursa which is nearer to Headford town and which indicates that they were both founded by St Furseus around 625 AD and before he set off for England in 637. This church may be the older of the two.

The much hidden east gable

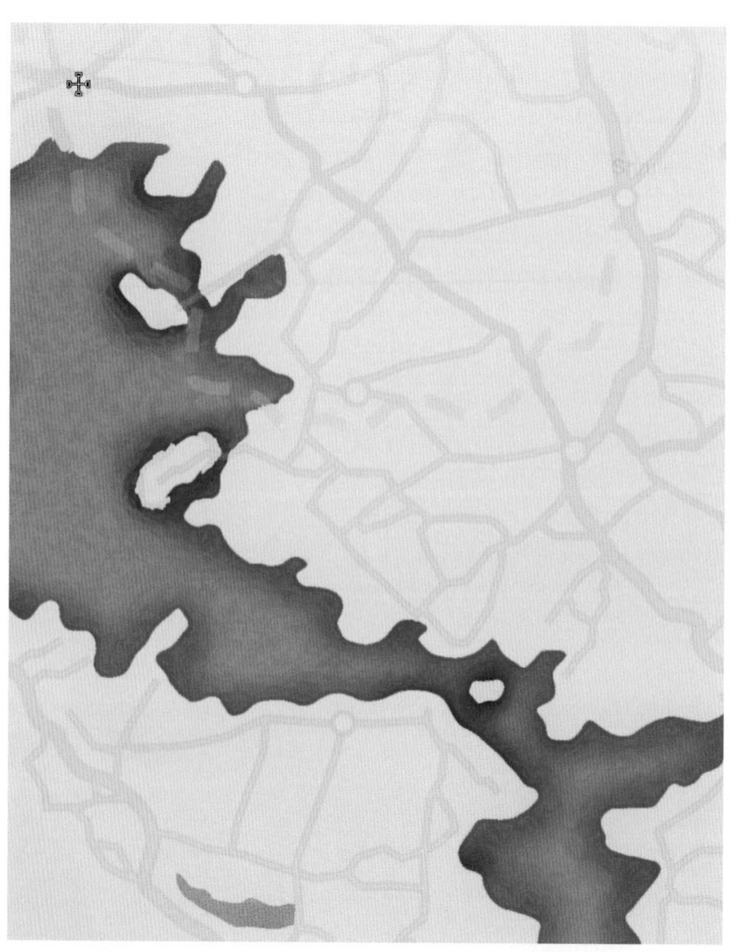

CONG

N53°32 W009°17

In the year 623 AD, St Feichin of the royal family of Finbar, who was born near Ballysodare in Co. Sligo, and educated by St Fintan, came to Cunga and founded a monastery a little to the south east of the present Abbey, and ever since Cong has been known in Irish as *Cunga Feicin* – Feichin's Neck of Land between the Waters. Of this foundation, which may have consisted of a small oratory and a few beehive dwelling huts, nothing now remains. He went on to found settlements on Omey and High Islands in Connemara which are described in *A Guide to Connemara's Early Christian Sites* (2008).

Cloister remains and west door to abbey

Feichin's abbey was destroyed by fire in the early 12th century but was refounded by Turlough Mór O'Connor, the High King of Ireland, ca. 1135. The Norman knight, William de Burgh, then attacked Cong in 1203, and again the abbey was rebuilt, possibly by Cathal O'Conor, the illegitimate son of Turloch Mór O'Conor, who came to the throne of Connacht in 1205.

above: Interior view of Cong Abbey below: External view

above: Monk's fishing house below: Stone carving of Rory O'Connor

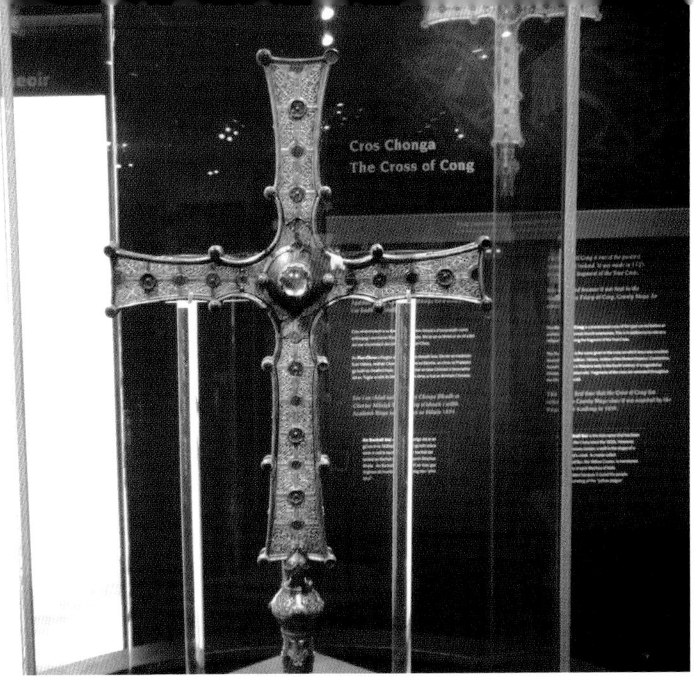

opposite page: West door into abbey above: Cross of Cong - photo courtesy of Oliver Previté

One of the most famous items of early Irish art is surely the beautiful Cross of Cong. This early medieval 12th century cross is an Irish Christian ornamental cross which was made for *Tairrdelbach Ua Conchobair* (1156 AD), King of Connacht and High King of Ireland to donate to St Mary's Cathedral in Tuam, Co. Galway. This cross was subsequently moved to Cong Abbey from which it takes its name. It was designed to be placed on the top of a staff and to hold a piece of the purported True Cross, which was to give it additional importance as an object of reverence.

At the time of writing, this cross is on display at the National Museum of Ireland - Country Life, Turlough, Castlebar, which is the first time it has been away from the National Museum of Ireland, Dublin, since the 1830s. It is considered to be one of the finest examples of metalwork and decorative art of its period in Western Europe.

Wilde says that St Fechin's church/oratory was dedicated to St Mary, as are both the Church of Ireland and Roman Catholic churches today.

IRISH MONASTIC OUTREACH

Many of the early monks referred to in this book were to follow that earlier injunction that encouraged the North African ascetics to ultimately leave family and clan so we find them and their followers venturing back into the wilds of Europe where they were to provide

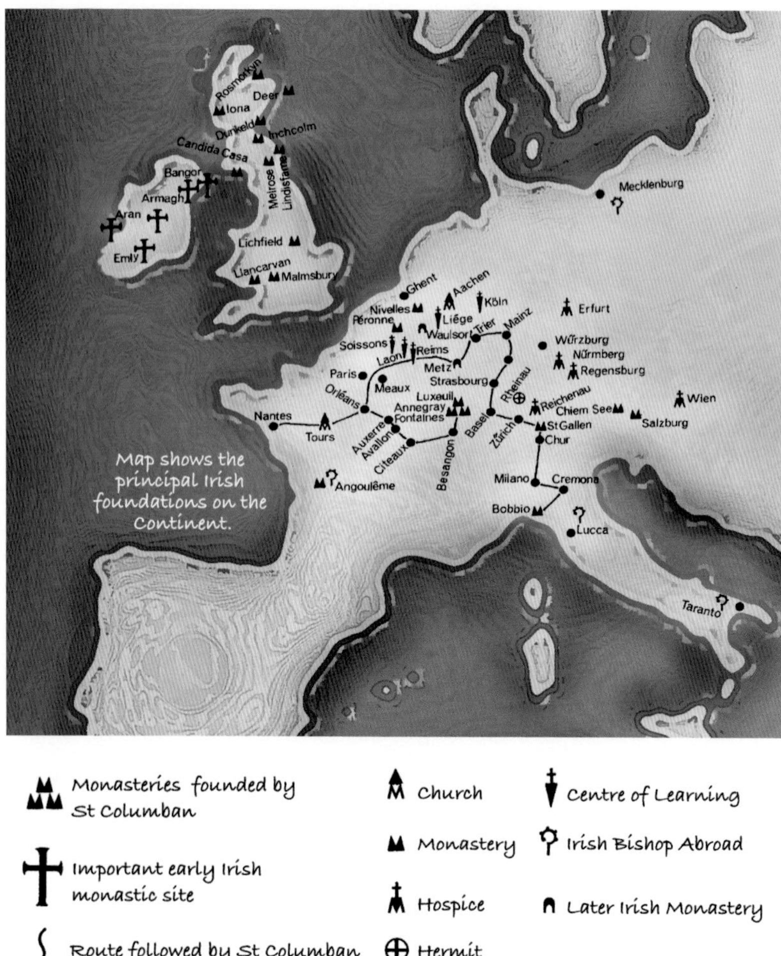

classical education and ultimately found so many of the well known monasteries such as at Louvain, Basel and Bobbio. An earlier chapter in this book describes the present day church at Fosses-la-Ville, which owes its foundation to St Faolan/Foillan from Inchiquinn. The accompanying map (*left page*) outlines an example of this amazing outreach alone through St Columban and his many followers. An expert on this particular aspect was the late Cardinal Tomás Ó Fiaich who travelled, wrote and lectured widely on the subject (*see Bibliography*).

This Irish monastic influence did indeed spread widely in Europe, first to Scotland and Northern England, then to Gaul and Italy. St Columba (*right*) and his followers established monasteries at Bangor, on the northeastern coast of Ireland, at Iona and then at Lindisfarne, which was founded by St Aidan, an Irish monk from Iona, at the request of King Oswald of Northumbria.

Illustration by John R Skelton (Columba banging on the gate of Bridei, son of Maelchon, King of Fortriu)

Then Columbanus, an abbot from a Leinster noble family, travelled to Gaul in the late 6th century with twelve companions also spreading this model of Irish monastic institutions throughout Europe. A whole new series of such foundations sprang up, starting with Fontaines and Luxeuil, being sponsored by the Frankish King Chilebert II. Following the king's death, Columbanus (picture on page 164 shows portrait in the stained glass window of the San Colombano Monastery in Bobbio, Italy) then went on to found a monastery at Metz, while one of his followers founded the monastery of St Gall on the shores of Lake Constance. Columbanus continued across the Alps into Italy where he established the monastery Bobbio. Amongst other well known names are Saints

Brendan, Comgall, Fergal, Gall, Dungal, Finian and then also St Boniface who was in fact English but was educated in Ireland at Lismore. The Irish had founded some 80 monastic centres in Ireland, Scotland, Northumbria and Wales. Some of these larger centres with maybe 200 or more monks.

According to the historian Paul Gallagher, between 575 and 725 in Continental Europe, the Irish monastic movement had founded 113 monasteries and schools in France and Switzerland, 26 in Germany, 10 in Austria and 3 in the north of Italy.

This monastic outreach has united Irish connections with Europe since the earliest times and should be something to be valued, remembered and celebrated in the same way that such European foundations celebrate their ancient origins in this country.

Portrait of Columbanus in the stained glass window of the San Colombano Monastery in Bobbio, Italy

Glossary

Antae A stone or wooden projection from the top of a side wall.

Aumbry A niche in the wall adjacent to the altar for storage of sacred communion vessels.

Batter The sloping inwards, from bottom to top, of a wall face.

Bullaun An artificial basin-like hollow in a stone or boulder, used for grinding corn. Mostly found in early monastic sites.

Byzantine Architectural style developed in the eastern European Roman Empire of Byzantium.

Chevron A triangulated stonework with the V shape pointing up or more often, down.

Clochán A corbel-roofed hut of dry stone, usually beehive-shaped.

Colonnettes Small arrangements of columns.

Cyclopean A style of stone walling where the stones cut into each other.

Finial Decorative fixture at the end and apex of a roof, sometimes in the form of a cross or figure, and depicting a monk/saint to whom the chapel was dedicated.

Garderobe A primitive toilet in a castle or other medieval structure, discharging to the outside.

Ogee A moulding with the profile of an S shaped curve.

Piers Raised supporting structures.

Pilaster Rectangular columns fastened into a wall.

Skewback The surface on which an arch joins the supporting abutment.

Trabeate Having a straight single stone lintel.

Voussoir One of the wedge-shaped stones of an arch.

Zoomorphic Representation of nature or animal forms being attributed to something, especially a deity.

Bibliography / Further Reading

Chadwick, Nora, *The Age of the Saints in the Early Celtic Church*, OUP, London 1963

Hayward, Richard, *The Corrib Country*, Dundalgan Press 1968

Killanin, Michael, & Duignan, Michael V, *Shell Guide to Ireland*, Ebury Press 1967

Leask, Harold G., *Irish Churches and Monastic Buildings*, Dundalgan Press 1996

Lewis, Samuel, *Topographical Dictionary of Ireland*, S. Lewis & Co, London 1837

MacManus, Declan, *A Guide to Ogham* 1994

Mitchell, Frank, & Ryan, Michael, *Reading the Irish Landscape*, Town House 2007

Office of Public Works, *Archaeological Inventory of Co. Galway, Vol 1 West Galway* 1993

Office of Public Works, *Archaeological Inventory of Co. Galway, Vol II North Galway* 1999

Ó Fiaich, Tomás, *Irish Cultural Influence in Europe, 6th to 12th century*, Dublin 1967

Ó Fiaich, Tomás, *Columbanus in His Own Words*, Veritas, Dublin 1974

Previté, Anthony, *A Guide to Connemara's Early Christian Sites*, Oldchapel Press 2008

Quinn, Bob, *Atlantean Irish, Ireland's Oriental & Maritime Heritage*, Lilliput Press, Dublin 2005

Ryan, John, *Irish Monasticism, Origins and Early Development*, First Published 1931

Rynne, Etienne, *The Luguaedon Pillar Stone, Journal of the Galway Archaeological and Historical Society* (pp. 205-211) 1995

Wilde, William, *Lough Corrib, Its Shores and Islands*, McGlashen & Gill 1867

INDEX

Queens

References

Also by this author

A Guide to Connemara's Early Christian Sites

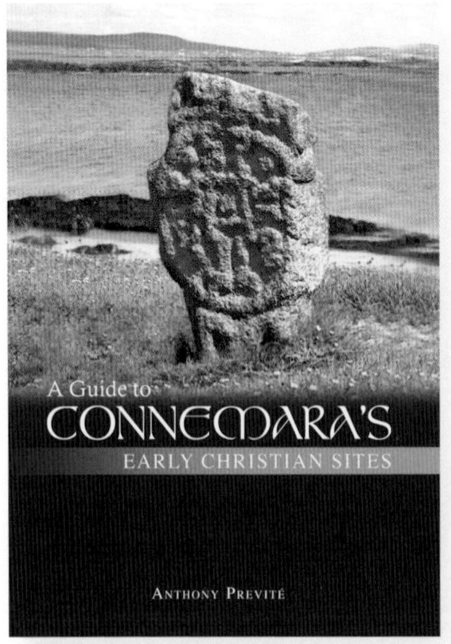

The islands and coastline of Connemara are alive with the constantly changing colours, clouds, sunlight or rain, sometimes disappearing and reappearing from blankets of sea fog and squalls of rain. The winter storms then purging the landscapes before the arrival of Spring. It was with such a kaleidoscope of seasons that the monks and eremitics of these often isolated and precarious sites lived their lives on the edge of what was a maritime highway reaching from North Africa to Scandinavia. It was these who introduced the spiritual traditions into Gaelic society as founded by the ascetics of the 3rd and 4th centuries.

So, the purpose of this little publication is in part a response to the frequently asked questions relating to the arrival of Christianity on our shores, and also to awaken an awareness of and to introduce the reader to the valuable history and heritage signified by these many coastal sites that surround the shores of Connemara.

In cases such as High Island and MacDara's Island this heritage has been well recognised and the ancient remains either restored or preserved and much valuable archaeological work undertaken. In other cases the remains are sadly disappearing or being destroyed through neglect or careless vandalism.

This book is primarily a guide to these unique sites of the past, yet not an academic research. Readers will hopefully further their interest with considerable benefit by consulting the acknowledged experts referred to in the bibliography such as Tim Robinson, Bob Quinn, Jenny White Marshall, Grellan D Rourke, etc., who have researched and contributed so widely to this subject.

First Published in 2008. ISBN 978-0-9560062-0-2. Please visit www.oldchapelpress.net